Between Jesus and the Black Dog

Between Jesus and the Black Dog

Christian Faith and Depression

Michael Rothery

and Anne-Marie McLaughlin

WIPF & STOCK · Eugene, Oregon

Wipf & Stock
An Imprint of Wipf and Stock Publishers
199 W. 8th Ave., Suite 3
Eugene, OR 97401

www.wipfandstock.com

PAPERBACK ISBN: 978-1-6667-0138-8
HARDCOVER ISBN: 978-1-6667-0139-5
EBOOK ISBN: 978-1-6667-0140-1

JUNE 22, 2021

Michael: To my wife Leslie Tutty,
with my deepest love and gratitude.

Anne-Marie: In memory of my father,
Jack McLaughlin.

The black dog I hope always to resist. . . .What shall exclude the black dog from a habitation such as this?

—SAMUEL JOHNSON, *on his attacks of melancholia.*

Contents

Acknowledgements | ix

1 | Introduction: On Being Christian
and Being Depressed | 1

    Stigma
    Stigma and Compassion
    Faith and Spiritual Commitments: Good News and Bad
    The Purpose of This Book: What and Whom It Is For
    Caveat: What This Book Is Not
    Praise for Fuzzy Concepts
    Reflection
    Reader Reflections

2 | Human Flourishing in a Problematic World | 13

    Stories: The Stuff of Life
    Flourishing and Creativity
    Flourishing in the Real (Broken) World
    Reader Reflections

3 | Depression: What It Is and Its Many Roots | 20

    What Depression Is
    What Causes Depression and How It Is Treated
    Alienation and Nihilism
    Social Isolation and Resources
    Reader Reflections

4 | SIN, REPENTANCE, AND FORGIVENESS | 31

    Sin

    Repentance

    Forgiveness

    On Forgiving Oneself

    Reader Reflections

5 | NARRATIVES ABOUT PERFECTIONISM
GUILT, SHAME, AND REDEMPTION | 39

    The Perfectionist's Narrative

    Sin and Redemption

    Acceptance

    Perfectionism and Self-Forgiveness

    Perfectionism and Narratives about Oneself

    Narrative Options

    Perfectionism and Narratives about Change

    Goals: Beyond Happiness

    Reader Reflections

6 | TRAUMA | 53

    Varieties of Traumatic Experience

    Trauma and Depression

    The Problem of Evil

    Trauma: The Narrative Challenge

    Trauma and Measured Forgiveness

    Spiritual and Religious Abuse

    Reader Reflections

7 | SPIRITUAL PRACTICES | 65

    The God Hypothesis

    Other People and Solitude

    Corporate and Personal Prayer

    Meditation and Contemplative Prayer

    Practice Options: Francesca's Journal

    Depression's Many Roots

    Spiritual Autobiography

Reader Reflections

8 | LOVE | 74

    The "L" Word
    Love of Oneself
    Love and Other People
    Love and God
    Reader Reflections

9 | EPILOGUE | 83

    The Complex Nature of the Black Dog
    Our Goals for This Book Revisited
    Reductionism
    Hope

Bibliography | 89

Acknowledgements

THERE ARE FRIENDS AND colleagues who were kind (and patient) enough to read parts of this work at earlier stages in its development. Many thanks for valuable feedback and consultation are extended to Fred Bonnell, Sue Gallagher, Glenn Hallgrimson, Mark McLaughlin, Dennis Morrison, Serena Patterson, Jason Rothery, Hilary Walsh, Richard Walsh, and Gordon Weber. "Francesca's" extensive influence on and contribution to the book will be obvious to the reader— her resilience, generosity, and intelligence could not be more deeply appreciated. Generations of students and clients have made an invaluable contribution to our thinking over many years, and to them we are also forever grateful.

The book is not quite perfect (see chapter 5); for any inevitable weaknesses and glitches, the authors take sole responsibility.

1

Introduction

On Being Christian and Being Depressed

Religious belief can be very close to madness. It has brought human beings to acts of criminal folly as well as to the highest achievements of goodness, creativity and generosity.[1]

No decent clinician avoids the most private and sensitive of topics; love, sex, death, jealousy, violence, addictions and betrayal are grist for the therapist's mill. Questions about spirituality and religion, however, are routinely neglected.[2]

"THEN I WAS THE most miserable person on earth, day and night was pure howling and despair," writes one of the most influential people in the history of Western Christianity. Martin Luther was subject to bouts of depression, which he called *"Anfechtungen* . . . or spiritual attacks,"[3] and he was not an anomaly. "Why are you cast down, O my soul, and why are you disquieted within me?" complains a psalmist.[4] "Out of the depths I cry to you, O

1. MacCulloch, *Christianity*, 13.

2. Pargament, *Spiritually Integrated Psychotherapy*, 7.

3. Roper, *Martin Luther*, 59.

4. Psalm 42:5.

Lord"[5] could serve as a mantra for contemporary Christians with depression on their bad days. "My soul is bereft of peace; I have forgotten what happiness is," writes the author of Lamentations,[6] words that reverberate in our communities' hospitals and clinics millennia later. Scores of similar examples could be cited, and being depressed, which is always painful for the afflicted, can be doubly difficult for people of faith.

Stigma

We stigmatize other people when we identify them as being somehow shameful, shame being *"the intensely painful feeling or experience of believing that we are flawed and therefore unworthy of love and belonging."*[7]

In very many cultures stigma compounds the distress of mental illness in general, and of depression specifically. In this regard having depression is not at all like having the flu—it is more often something to hide to avoid awkward embarrassment, or other (sometimes worse) social consequences.

For Christians who are depressed the problem of stigma is especially complicated. "I realized," writes Fawcett, "there was a stigma associated with depression; many saw it as a character flaw or weakness. . . . The more I listened and the more I read, I also came to understand that the stigma was strong among Christians."[8] The extra complication comes with the expectation that one should always be a good ambassador, selling the advantages of a Christian life. Optics are therefore important: "I considered it my responsibility to look like a winner, maintain the image, and try to make my life appear problem-free, as if I were a walking billboard

---

5. Psalm 130:1.
6. Lamentations 3:17.
7. Brown, *Gifts of Imperfection*, 39.
8. Fawcett, *Hope for Wholeness*, 31.

advertising that perfect, painless lives were the product of a relationship with Christ."[9]

A resource we will frequently rely on in this book is the personal journal of a woman whose story includes sexual abuse as a child, an addiction to alcohol from her teens through age thirty-five, and chronic depression. Stigma being as it is, she has chosen to protect herself by remaining anonymous, adopting "Francesca" as her *nom de plume*.

Through the influence of Sandy,[10] her partner of many years, Francesca's remarkable resilience in the face of ominous odds involved, among many other things, joining a church. The congregation was predominantly liberal, and Francesca found it ironic that her lesbian relationship was never an issue, while her struggles with depression occasionally were. An entry in her journal reads:

> My taking Prozac was a big deal for some people. They showed me they were upset by making jokes that weren't funny—stuff like that. One man finally told me he had trouble "believing in" depression! I thought that was weird, considering I could never make it all up. I told him I didn't think his attitude was very Christian.

Of course, one needn't go to church to have such experiences:

> At a dinner party I go to, the subject of antidepressants comes up and an excoriating critique of them . . . is quoted approvingly by several of the people present. . . . As I listen to the conversation I sense an unspoken investment in holding depression up to censure, as though it were still, after all these years, a fraudulent bundle of symptoms, an inflated case of malingering that everyone suffers from but that only a select, self-indulgent few choose to make a big deal about. No wonder people keep it a secret.[11]

---

9. Fawcett, *Hope for Wholeness*, 45.

10. Of course, another assumed name.

11. Merkin, *This Close to Happy*, 125.

We have said that being depressed can be especially difficult for Christians (and people in other spiritual communities); this is due to the *double stigma* such people can experience. There is the stigma that everyone with mental health issues will encounter. Added to this is the special shame that comes with being a depressed *Christian*; not only is one suspected of being a "fraudulent bundle of symptoms," but one is also weak in one's faith—why else would one succumb to deep unhappiness?

Stigma and Compassion

An important fact about stigma is that it is antithetical to compassion. When we stigmatize others, we tend to withhold compassion that we would otherwise feel. To the extent that we stigmatize depressed people, we will be slow to feel sorry about their condition, and to proffer appropriate help and support. Conversely, if we do *not* stigmatize people with depression, we are more likely to be open to their pain and to be helpful to them.

By Nussbaum's account[12] we experience compassion when we observe someone (Francesca, for example) in distress, consider that her suffering is significant, determine that we cannot dismiss her suffering by arguing she brought it on herself, and view her as a sufficiently important person. This last criterion means that we empathize with Francesca enough that her suffering matters to us (our capacity for empathy is strong enough, and Francesca is a person who is important enough to us for us to engage with her empathically).

Albert Einstein is credited with originating the circle of compassion metaphor, suggesting that we all draw imaginary circles that encompass some people while excluding (often stigmatizing) others. An example painfully familiar to most is the ingroup/outgroup phenomenon that is the bane of many a high school student's social existence. But the dynamic is not restricted to the world of

---

12. Nussbaum, *Upheavals of Thought*, 335; see also Nussbaum, *Anger and Forgiveness*, 23.

adolescence—it is seen throughout life, and the consequences can be extremely serious.

Someone who strongly stigmatizes people like Francesca who have depressive disorders will place them outside his or her circle of compassion, and will tend to be unconcerned about their needs and welfare—perhaps dismissing them as an "inflated case of malingering that everyone suffers from but that only a select, self-indulgent few choose to make a big deal about."[13] The same person might have similarly negative, stigmatizing attitudes toward homeless people who are addicted to alcohol, and he or she might tend to stereotype women or gay people in ways that disadvantage them. In each case (and there are variations in degree involved) the consequence is that compassion is to some extent withheld: defining someone as an "inflated case of malingering" means there is no need to take that person's pain seriously, or to advocate for services to alleviate that person's distress.

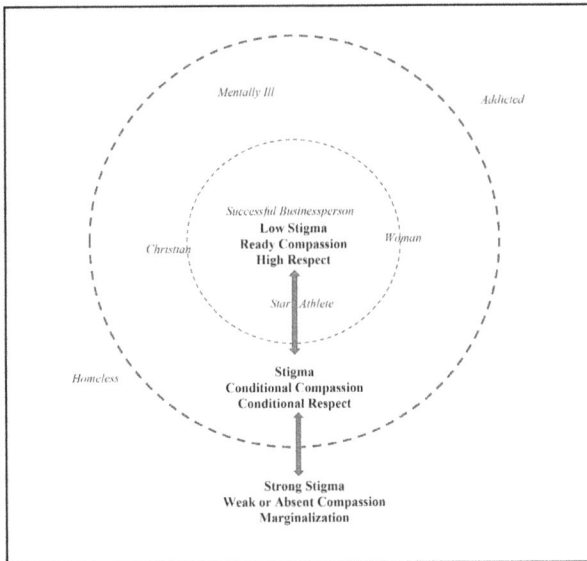

The example in the figure above represents one possible person's position at one point in time, and it does not capture an

13. Again, see Merkin, *This Close to Happy*, 125.

important piece of information—we make judgements about ourselves as we do about others, and these judgements can be especially problematic for Christians with depression: "When a person already is depressed, religious beliefs can irrationally amplify guilt, apathy, or self-hatred . . . Those with psychiatric disorders suffer daily, often in ways hidden to others around them, and religious faith sometimes exacerbates this suffering instead of lessening it."[14]

Faith and Spiritual Commitments: Good News and Bad

The purpose of this book is to explore the relationship between Christian belief and the experience of depression, including the tasks associated with effectively managing this common problem. The good news is that Christianity and other religions can have beneficial effects on a broad range of health issues, and we will be focusing in the pages that follow on dozens of ideas about how religion can help the healing process. However, we would be remiss if we ignored ways in which it can also make things worse. It will be important as we proceed to recognize potential bad news: "Examples are easy to find to argue that religion is either humankind's greatest gift or its greatest curse," Griffith asserts.[15] At the same time as we draw on Christianity's contribution to healing from depression, we will consider risks it can pose. Christians with depression can treat themselves badly, just as they can be unreasonably negative in their attitudes toward other people. For example, religion can isolate people in their own limited group and motivate them to deny compassion to many others.

Fortunately, there is good news enough to counterbalance the bad. Most Christians would agree with Griffith about the importance of several essential and positive Christian values:[16]

---

14. Griffith, *Religion that Heals, Religion that Harms*, 8.

15. Griffith, *Religion that Heals, Religion that Harms*, 3.

16. See Griffith, *Religion that Heals, Religion that Harms*, 29–30.

* relationships which recognize the depth and complexity of other people,

* compassion toward other people,

* compassion toward oneself,

* hopeful resilience,

* a personal sense of the sacred,

* making the needs of individual people more important than the needs of a religious group.

In general, reviews of research conclude that there is significant scientific support for claiming that measurable benefits (including decreased depression) flow from spiritual practices:

> Several studies have found that hopefulness and a sense that life is meaningful are essential to mental and physical well-being and are a major ingredient in a person's resiliency in the face of crisis, illness, and suffering. Studies consistently show that those who are able to draw comfort and meaning from their religion and employ some spiritual discipline regularly have lower levels of psychological distress, better adjustment, and less anxiety and depression, even when their social and economic status and their general health conditions are taken into account.[17]

The Purpose of This Book: What and Whom It Is For

As stated above, the purpose of this book is to explore the relationship between Christian belief and the experience of depression. We will be discussing strengths and benefits that come with Christian faith and can help achieve the goal of managing depression's deleterious effects. It has been written with Christians experiencing depressive disorders in mind, and the hope was always that it would also be of interest to their friends, loved ones, and mental

17. Jones, *Mirror of God*, Kindle loc. 1668–76; see also Pargament, *Spiritually Integrated Psychotherapy*, 90.

health professionals. The latter group is living through a change whereby the traditional professional stance toward clients' spiritual beliefs and commitments—to politely ignore them—is being openly challenged by a new perspective. Increasingly, as religious/spiritual beliefs and practices are understood to be a critical part of many clients' frames of reference, the emphasis is on respecting and utilizing those beliefs and practices rather than excluding them from the important work of counseling and psychotherapy.

Chapter 2, following these introductory comments, is "Human Flourishing in a Problematic World." It begins with the introduction of the popular metaphor of our lives as stories or narratives. Who we are, our identity, is the complex product of a creative process. In an important sense, our lives are *authored* by us, forged from our experiences—the good news and bad that awaits us from birth and out of which we must make sense.

The woman whose life is referenced throughout the book, Francesca, shares a narrative about sexual abuse, alcoholism, and depression, but it is also about her resilience, and an important part of her resilience is her Christianity. It is this critical narrative thread we begin with, starting with news about flourishing, about life lived with a fullness that can seem elusive to some of us some of the time.

Chapter 3 is "Depression: What It Is and Its Many Roots." As with other aspects of our life stories, depression is complex, like a plant with many roots.

We will demonstrate in chapter 3 that while depression may have one primary root cause, as often as not it has two or three or more different roots. When this is the case, it makes good sense to seek relief via multiple solutions, rather than putting all our eggs in one basket (however important that basket may be). The best outcomes are achieved when the complexity of depression is respected by coordinating, over time, a multifaceted response.

Sin is a concept that is (for better or for worse) critically important to Christians but tends to be avoided by non-religious people, including many who work in secular helping agencies—the latter may even consider preoccupations with sin to be irrational guilt, more likely to feed than to ameliorate depression. Narratives about sin (and also repentance and forgiveness) are the focus of chapter 4. Similarly, chapter 5 addresses perfectionism, a story that can make Christians vulnerable to depression given the wrong narrative context, perfectionism being a framework that fails to give enough weight to acceptance and forgiveness.

Trauma is recognized as a frequent source of depression and is singled out for special treatment in chapter 6, while chapter 7 is about spiritual practices (e.g., prayer) and their role in managing depression. Chapter 8 reflects on an all-important source of hope for meaning and relief of suffering, this being narratives about love. A brief epilogue concludes the work by anchoring three overarching themes that infuse this book throughout: complexity, reductionism, and hope.

Caveat: What This Book Is Not

This book is a supplement, not a substitute for professional help, including medical intervention and/or counseling with a qualified practitioner. Don't hesitate to consult with your doctor or another professional if you are distressed by symptoms of depression. Finding the right help is sometimes a challenge; be prepared to "shop" for someone who feels and looks like a good fit. If you suspect that child abuse, violent relationships, or any other trauma has contributed to your distress, discuss with potential helpers your need for expert aid focusing on this aspect of your history.

This book is not a substitute for the emotional support that comes from good relationships with friends and loved ones. If you do not have this resource in your life at this time, seek out counseling with someone who can help, and put loneliness on the list of issues you would like help with. It's not a good idea to go it alone.

If spiritual confusions and pain are part of what you are experiencing, spiritual direction is available in most communities. As with any potential resource, be prepared to talk to more than one person in your search for helpers who seem compatible and have the right expertise.

If you suspect you are self-medicating, using alcohol or other non-prescribed drugs to cope with emotional stress, make this a priority among the issues you want to work on.

If this all seems overly demanding, read through chapter 5 on perfectionism, and remind yourself that it's alright to accept the reality that progress is usually achieved a step at a time.

Praise for Fuzzy Concepts

It may be unnecessarily frustrating for some readers to find there are limits regarding how definitive we can be about what we mean when we speak about narratives, flourishing, creativity, depression, and mental health, to cite just a few examples. For each of these terms it is the case that however much we may act as if its meaning is clear to us, it is actually fuzzy. We know flourishing and creativity when we see strong, clear examples, but there are many less definitive cases where the boundary between flourishing versus languishing, or creativity versus a mundane predictability, no matter how carefully we define them, will always prove to be blurred.

This blurred-boundary issue, which is more common than we may recognize, was described by the Cambridge philosopher Ludwig Wittgenstein over sixty years ago:

> I am saying that these phenomena have no one thing in common which makes us use the same word for all,— but that they are *related* to one another in many different ways. . . . I can think of no better expression to characterize these similarities than 'family resemblances'; for the various resemblances between members of the family: Build, features, color of eyes, gait, temperament . . . overlap and crisscross in the same way.[18]

If we are uncomfortable with the thought that we cannot always say precisely what we are talking about, Wittgenstein recommends acceptance:

18. Wittgenstein, *Philosophical Investigations*, 27–28.

But this is not ignorance. We do not know the boundaries because none have been drawn. . . . We can draw a boundary—for a special purpose. Does it take that to make the concept usable? Not at all! . . . One might say that the concept . . . is a concept with blurred edges.—"But is a blurred concept a concept at all?"—Is an indistinct photograph a picture of a person at all? Is it even always an advantage to replace an indistinct picture with a sharp one? Isn't the indistinct one often exactly what we need?[19]

Reflection

Each chapter in this book concludes with an invitation to reflect upon its personal implications and narrative importance. This is in keeping with the fact that self-reflection is necessarily part of our spiritual development. Francesca reflected on her narrative choices in conversation with friends and loved ones, and also with professional helpers. Equally if not more important was her practice of journaling, a contemplative exercise that served her well over many years, one which is available to us all.

Meditation and contemplative prayer are practices that Francesca explored. Always, however, she returned to her journal—finding writing a useful discipline for clarifying and anchoring her thinking about her life's stories and their meaning respecting her drive to understand and flourish.

We will conclude each chapter in this book with a selection of questions that are offered as stimuli for useful reflection on what it has covered. Approach these exercises with a spirit of friendly curiosity, as a chance to expand your relationship with yourself (and perhaps with others as well).

19. Wittgenstein, *Philosophical Investigations*, 28–29.

Reader Reflections

In a spirit of friendly curiosity, discuss or write about any of the following reflections that look interesting to you:

1. Draw the circle of compassion presented in this introduction. Write descriptive words about yourself on it. Place these words where you think they belong on the circle. An important final instruction is this: if you haven't already done so, conclude the exercise by finding words that you place at the center of the circle, things that are deserving of deep respect and compassion.

2. Which approach or approaches to reflection do you favor? These could be journaling, contemplative prayer or meditation, discussing issues with trusted friends and/or loved ones, discussion with a professional helper, or anything else that appeals to you.

3. When have you been subjected to stigma? What was the issue around which you felt stigmatized and what was its effect on you? What if anything did you do about it?

4. Are there people you are slow to feel compassion for? What (if anything) might lead to a change of mind on your part respecting someone from that group of people?

5. Identify an important concept that is hard for you to define with absolute clarity (love, for example, or sin, or depression). What makes it important? What would be the consequences of trying to live without this concept?

2

HUMAN FLOURISHING IN A PROBLEMATIC WORLD

Humans cannot live without stories. We surround ourselves with them; we make them up in our sleep; we tell them to our children; we pay to have them told to us. . . . A few of us . . . spend our entire adult lives trying to understand their beauty, power, and influence.[1]

"Joy is a by-product," the Archbishop began. "If you set out and say, 'I want to be happy,' clenching your teeth with determination, this is the quickest way of missing the bus."[2]

THE ANTITHESIS TO DEPRESSION is not simple happiness, and some sort of pain-free existence is not what we mean by "flourishing." Martin Seligman[3] is writing for psychology (not a spiritually oriented audience) when he stipulates that "positive emotions" like happiness and joy are only one of at least five "elements" that make for "well-being," which is synonymous with flourishing. Other elements include:

* ✳ "Engagement" (which spiritually oriented readers can take to be commitment, an act of faith).

1. Greenblatt, *Rise and Fall of Adam and Eve*, 2.
2. Dali Lama, Tutu, and Abrams, *Book of Joy*, 193.
3. Seligman, *Hope Circuit*, 261.

* "Relationships" or a capacity for love.

* "Meaning," which refers to our ability to recognize the inherent value in things or events.

* "Accomplishment," which has such terms as "achievement," "mastery," and "competence" as frequent synonyms.

Shortly, we will expand on a Christian notion of flourishing being a larger and more basic life goal of which happiness is but a part—the creative challenge that faces us all is to author a story about our lives, a narrative that enables us to flourish in a flawed world. First, however, there is more to say about the idea of our lives as creative narratives.

Stories: The Stuff of Life

We will rely on a popular and useful metaphor in this book of our lives as narratives, or stories. Francesca, who was introduced in the previous chapter, has a complex understanding of her life's story and how it is unfolding. Like everyone's, her story is unique, but it draws on common, basic questions we all must answer, beginning when we are very young:

1. What sort of kid am I?

2. What is this world like?

3. What can I expect from other people?

4. What can I expect from God?

5. What does a kid like me do with her or his life, in a world like this, in the company of people like these, with the nature of God being what it is?

This is impressive, creative work, which begins in infancy and lasts a lifetime. Often the initial answers to the questions are simple, but we elaborate on them, adding complexity and richness as we grow, using whatever experiences we are offered or find for ourselves along the way.

Stories serve functions that are at once deeply personal, social, and cultural. They "provide meaning and explanation . . . [and] create bonds between people."[4] Further, "We have evolved a cultural world. Our collectively imagined ideas and concepts shape the very fabric of our reality."[5]

For most of us the stories we compose are a mix of good and bad news; hopefully the good outweighs the bad and our story is a positive one in balance, and we flourish. When we are less fortunate and the weight of the bad news is significant, life might be more difficult, as was Francesca's. Despite her history of childhood sexual abuse, however, and a time when she was addicted to alcohol and seriously depressed, Francesca was ultimately resilient. Her resilience is what we will focus on in this chapter; we will attend more to the bad news in the next, which is about depression's roots, and in chapter 6, which is about trauma.

Despite her difficulties learning to love and value herself, there came a point in a conversation with one of several therapists where Francesca added "survivor" to her answers to the question, "What sort of kid am I?" Despite a sometimes-overwhelming experience of her world being lonely, and empty of resources, she came slowly to acknowledge and appreciate its variety and even its hard-to-believe richness. In spite of powerful lessons about other people being dangerous and inflicting pain, she was able to find trust in caring relationships, one of them a committed life partnership. Reading Francesca's journal, one finds a footer at the bottom of every page, which reads: *Surrender to a stubborn God, and an easy affection for a mucked-up world.*[6] As an alternative to believing that God had abandoned her, Francesca drew the very different conclusion that God was "stubborn"—that is, that God seemed to be unconditionally committed to her for the long term.

---

4. Suddendorf, *Gap*, 222.

5. Suddendorf, *Gap*, 224.

6. The language Francesca sometimes used has been slightly sanitized. "Mucked-up" is not precisely what she wrote.

Flourishing and Creativity

In an admittedly fuzzy definition, "*Flourishing* . . . evokes an image of a living thing, thriving in its proper environment. . . . The good life consists not merely in succeeding in one or another endeavor we undertake . . . but in living into our human and personal fullness—that, in a word, is a flourishing life."[7] We would say Francesca was *flourishing* as a survivor once she reached the point in her life when she had a partner with whom she felt safe, a church that offered her hope and community, and professional help with coming to terms with her traumatic history—among other important resources. Describing her as flourishing means she is living into a creative and rewarding life.

Creativity is the innovative and effective exercise of free will in pursuit of value.[8] When we say Francesca is creative, we are recognizing a strength that characterizes the lives of all ordinary people, not just of an exceptional and gifted minority:

> Creativity shouldn't be seen as something otherworldly. It shouldn't be thought of as a process reserved for artists and inventors and other "creative types." The human mind, after all, has the creative impulse built into its operating system, hard-wired into its most essential programming code. At any given moment, the brain is automatically forming new associations, continually connecting an everyday x to an unexpected y.[9]

As we have noted, one of the tasks this remarkable brain undertakes is authoring a life narrative—in the process of accomplishing the same feat as Francesca achieved.

---

7. Volf, *Flourishing*, ix.

8. Note that value can be moral, aesthetic, and epistemic—creativity will change flavor with shifts in the balance of priorities. A creative philosopher is after epistemic value (truth) and, perhaps, also moral value (ethics); Bach, the ultimate example of a creative genius, writing spiritually profound music, was after all three types, with a strong emphasis on epistemic (truth) and aesthetic (beauty).

9. Lehrer, *Imagine*, Kindle loc. 208–12.

Flourishing in the Real (Broken) World

Christians dealing with depression are faced with two questions, both of them legitimate, which point in opposite directions. The first is: How can I be a good enough Christian and be depressed? The second is: How can I be a good enough Christian and *not* be depressed? The challenge contained in the first question is that if we believe in a loving God, we should not be filled with despair. If we are, that implies a lack of faith. It is symptomatic of a spiritual flaw. The challenge contained in the second question is the idea that we can only be undepressed—joyful and happy—if we are willfully deaf to stories about suffering, our own and others'. Do compassion and happiness mutually exclude one another?

> How can we laugh and rejoice, when there are so many tears to be wiped away and when new tears are being added every day? . . . How can one rejoice when innocent people are killed . . . when children are starving in Africa? . . . Don't we live in one world? Do we have a right to joy if we do not cry out for those who suffer?[10]

This is, as noted, a genuine conundrum—both seemingly contradictory questions are legitimate.

Desmond Tutu, a prominent Christian, and the Dalai Lama, a famous Buddhist, are friends who wrote a book, together with Douglas Abrams, about flourishing. These individuals are not blind to Moltmann's ubiquitous tears. Desmond Tutu, in the aftermath to apartheid in South Africa, chaired the Truth and Reconciliation Commission. He and his colleagues confronted deep evil while inviting stories about the suffering racist people have visited on their victims. The Dalai Lama fled the Chinese invasion of Tibet; he and his followers continue to live in exile decades later. And yet, he and Desmond Tutu teamed up to write *The Book of Joy: Lasting Happiness in a Changing World*. In it, they describe a survey they conducted: "We invited the world to ask their questions about joy, and . . . we received more than a thousand. It was fascinating that the most asked question was not about how we could discover our

10. Moltmann, *Christianity*, 1–2.

own joy but how we could possibly live with joy in a world filled with so much suffering."[11]

Part of being fully human—certainly Christian—is accepting that flourishing is not a happiness that in any way supplants pain:

> But are joy and protest, happiness and pain, laughter and tears true alternatives? I don't believe they are. The secret of life is *love*. In love we go out of ourselves and lay ourselves open to all the experiences of life. In the love of life we become happy and vulnerable at the same time. In love we can be happy and sad. . . . In love we can rejoice and must protest at the same time. The more deeply love draws us into life, the more alive and, simultaneously, the more capable of sorrow we become. That is the dialectic of the affirmed and loved life. We can't have the first without the second.[12]

Pennington concurs: "Human flourishing is experienced now in the midst of suffering and the brokenness of the world. . . . Human flourishing will only be experienced in a paradoxical way that combines loss, longing, suffering, and persecution with true happiness, joy, satisfaction, and peace."[13]

Discussions of evil often invoke, as stark examples, the holocaust in Nazi Germany and sadistic child abuse (often as chillingly portrayed by Dostoevsky in *The Brothers Karamazov*). Moltmann contrasts the latter with the "Ode to Joy," the text famously used by Beethoven in his triumphant Ninth Symphony:

> This means that Schiller's "Ode to Joy" and Dostoevsky's indignation about the innocent suffering of the child are not in fact antitheses, and we don't have to choose between them. Joy in life's happiness motivates us to revolt against the life that is destroyed and against those who destroy life. And the grief over life that is destroyed is nothing other than an ardent longing for life's liberation to happiness and joy. Otherwise we would accept

11. Dalai Lama, Tutu, and Abrams, *Book of Joy*, 7.

12. Moltmann, *Christianity*, 14.

13. Pennington, *Sermon on the Mount and Human Flourishing*, 296.

innocent suffering and destroyed life as our fate and destiny. Compassion is the other side of the living joy. We don't accuse God because there is suffering in the world. Rather, we protest in the name of God against suffering and those who cause it.[14]

This "protest in the name of God" is one of two focuses that Christian priorities entail: "an authentic faith is always engaged, at work to relieve personal suffering as well as to push against social injustice, political violence, and environmental degradation."[15]

Reader Reflections

In a spirit of friendly curiosity, write or talk about any of the following reflections that look interesting to you:

1. What is your favorite example of your own creativity?

2. Do you think your creativity has anything to do with God? Elaborate.

3. What aspects of your life do you consider to be examples of flourishing?

4. In your mind, are flourishing and happiness basically the same thing? Is there a point to treating them like separate concepts?

5. Imagine you could have met with the Dalai Lama and/or Desmond Tutu when they were working on their book. What would you say to them about being happy in today's world?

14. Moltmann, *Christianity*, 14; on the frequently tragic side to human lives see also Harries, *Beauty and the Horror*, especially ch. 16.

15. Volf, *Flourishing*, 9.

3

DEPRESSION

What It Is and Its Many Roots

In sooth, I know not why I am so sad.
It wearies me, you say it wearies you,
But how I caught it, found it, or came by it,
Which stuff 'tis made of, whereof it is born
I am to learn;
And such a want-wit sadness makes of me
That I have much ado to know myself.[1]

FRANCESCA'S NARRATIVE, AS INDICATED earlier, is about resilience, a survivor's story in which she creates a valued life for herself despite sexual abuse at the hands of her father when she was very young—so young that her earliest memories are stored and recalled as strong emotional and physical reactions, inchoate recollections that distressed and confused her. She has more concrete memories of her painful teenage years and recalled them in her journal:

> Part of me was desperate for explanations, but mostly I
> felt completely hopeless. The possibility of ever finding
> something in myself that's worth anything seemed about

1. Shakespeare, *Merchant of Venice*, 1.1.1–7.

zero. I hated myself like I thought my father did. There was nothing I *did* that I could hate myself for, really. I could write down a list of hateful things, but they were about who I *was* rather than things I did. Acts can be forgiven but being just a worthless person can't.

Francesca goes on to reference her efforts to "drown" herself by drinking, with alcoholism beginning in her mid-teens and a subsequent diagnosis of depression:

When I was told I was an alcoholic I argued the point, but I wasn't really surprised. When she [a nurse] told me I was depressed, I didn't know what she meant exactly . . . I knew I felt like crap most of the time but had never named it until she fetched a book and went over a list of symptoms, and I had to admit they sounded a lot like me. A nice way of telling me I'm mucked up, I thought. Along with drinking too much I was a case of muckupedness[2] in a book. Pretty soon I actually felt ok about that—sort of. It was better than feeling all alone.

What Depression Is

The book Francesca's nurse used was likely an early version of the American Psychiatric Association's *Diagnostic and Statistical Manual of Mental Disorders* (DSM), with criteria for depression very similar to those in the current fifth edition, the DSM-5.[3]

* She would have been asked if she suffered from a "depressed mood" most of the time.

* Did she find she did not enjoy life as much as she should, given her circumstances?

* Did she have little or no appetite for food (or, on the other hand, a frequent urge to overeat)?

2. As noted in the previous chapter, we have on occasion slightly edited Francesca's language.

3. American Psychiatric Association, *Diagnostic and Statistical Manual of Mental Disorders*, 160–61.

* Did she often have insomnia (or, alternatively, a tendency to sleep too much)?

* Did she find she was restless most days, or was she slowed down, with feelings of lassitude?

* Did she feel tired much of the time?

* Did she frequently have unreasonable feelings of guilt or shame, or worthlessness?

* Was she experiencing problems concentrating and decision-making?

* Was she often preoccupied with death, which could include suicidal thoughts or attempts?

Of course, answering yes to some of these questions at times is entirely normal: one might be simply having a bad day, or under stress, or coping with a loss—it's important to recognize that there are questions of degree, frequency, and circumstance that determine whether a person is or isn't likely experiencing a depressive disorder (of which there are many variations). However, as we emphasized in our introduction, it is also important to consult your doctor or other professional if you are at all concerned.

In Francesca's case there was little question about whether the criteria were a fit for her or not. She was seriously depressed, at the same time as she was drinking far too much alcohol, an effort at self-medication that was making things worse. Whether she drank because she was depressed or was depressed because she drank is not terribly important; each problem contributed to the other, and both were rooted in the severe trauma that a sexual abuse history necessarily represents.

We have suggested that we all make sense of our experience by creating narratives. The symptoms listed in manuals like the DSM-5 serve a useful purpose but suggest little about *why* Francesca's life followed its dangerous path or what she was eventually able to do to correct that. These questions are only answerable if we understand what Francesca's unhappy early life meant to her— what narrative sense did she make of it all, and how did that shape her subsequent experience? Francesca's journal, written over many years, is a lengthy document and is a resource on which we will draw as we explore her story. We will have to be selective as we consider information from her journal relevant to the five basic narrative questions introduced in chapter 2 and as we add depth and detail to each.

What sort of kid am I? Recalling her late teens, Francesca wrote about feeling powerless, worthless, and shameful. For some reason, most abused children feel they are responsible for their own victimization, and Francesca was no exception. "I don't think it made sense," she wrote, "but part of me was totally sure I was to blame. I just *believed* what was done to me would not have happened if I was a good enough girl." She felt trapped in a deep sense of her own worthlessness, claiming she would like to be "anybody but me, any place but this, any time but now."

What is this world like? The place Francesca wished she were free of was a dangerous world, empty of hope.

What can I expect from other people? "I remember thinking that my life was something that could be taken away from me if he wanted, and nobody would care enough to do anything." Some people inflicted enormous pain and suffering, while others were indifferent, or powerless to protect her.

What can I expect from God? "We went to church when I was growing up. Sometimes I felt mad at God but also wanted to cry. One of my counselors once asked me what I had thought God would do for me, and the answer was nothing. God was either helpless or didn't care. The counselor said I must have felt like God abandoned me, and that's a good word for it."

What does a kid like me do with his or her life, in a world like this, in the company of people like these, with the nature of God being what it is? Recalling her father hitting her so hard she just about tumbled down a flight of stairs, and considered letting herself fall, she writes: "I didn't let go. . . . I hung on. I'm still not one to let go. . . . [Even though] I expected to die a failure. Drinking is one way to do this."

What Causes Depression and How It Is Treated

The psychiatric nurse who introduced Francesca to the DSM criteria for depression initiated an important conversation that would continue for several years and include many people. As she struggled to come to grips with her deep pain, she inevitably encountered different narratives regarding what depression is and what causes it, and what can be done to alleviate its suffering.

One prominent school of thought sees depression as primarily a biological problem, an issue with brain chemistry gone awry—with the treatment of choice being drugs that work to restore a subtle chemical balance. Not everyone applauds this point of view; in fact, there are insistent voices arguing that it is at best sorely inadequate:

> You aren't a machine with broken parts. You are an animal whose needs are not being met. You need to have a community. You need to have meaningful values, not the junk values you've been pumped full of all your life, telling you happiness comes through money and buying objects. You need to have meaningful work. You need the natural world. You need to feel you are respected. You need a secure future. You need connections to all these things. You need to release any shame you might feel for having been mistreated.
> . . . You are not suffering from a chemical imbalance in your brain. You are suffering from a social and spiritual imbalance in how we live.[4]

It would be entirely possible for Francesca, if she sought relief in her younger days, to encounter professional helpers whose priority would not be to address her history of abuse, but to find the best medication(s) at the optimal dosage to help her feel better and get on with her life. For very many depressed people, such a medical approach is helpful, even essential, but not sufficient.[5]

4. Hari, *Uncovering the Real Causes of Depression*, 255.

5. E.g., Solomon, *Noonday Demon*. Readers with a scientific background may be interested in Cipriani et al., "Comparative Efficacy and Acceptability of 21 Antidepressant Drugs"; and Hieronymus et al., "Consistent Superiority of

On her path to resilience, Francesca did make long-term use of antidepressant drugs; she also received counseling from a variety of sources. Not surprisingly given its popularity and empirical status, a number of the professionals she consulted worked from a cognitive-behavioral therapy (CBT) framework. By these professionals, the ongoing cause of Francesca's depression was seen as problematic beliefs and related behaviors, and treatment involved exploring and modifying the beliefs she harbored respecting her worthlessness, the dangerousness of other people, and the bleakness of her world, empty of the resources one needs to flourish.[6]

It should be emphasized that depression is often caused by painful current circumstances. Being in violent or in other ways troubled intimate relationships, or stuck in a job in which one is being mistreated or feels dead-ended, or suffering a significant loss, or chronic difficulties with health—these are all examples of circumstances that should be addressed when improvements are possible. Had Francesca received help when she was still being sexually abused, relying exclusively on medications or CBT would be a very serious error—it could even make her depression worse. There are myriad similar examples, such as poverty, social isolation, substance abuse (which can cause or exacerbate depression), or demanding caretaking responsibilities from which there is no sufficient relief.

Spiritual crises and conflicts are often deeply troubling, and they can be a primary cause of depression. In Francesca's case, depression's roots were obviously embedded in her sexual abuse history. Also, however, she writes, "My anger and feelings of abandonment by God were a result of the abuse. I always point at that when I'm asked what the main cause of my depression was. But I also say that for getting control and managing my muckupedness, getting a handle on my angry feelings toward God has been huge."

Selective Serotonin Reuptake Inhibitors over Placebo," for meta-analytic studies that support the use of antidepressant medications.

6. See Pearce, *Cognitive Behavioral Therapy for Christians with Depression.*

Alienation and Nihilism

The roots of depression are truly diverse, so much so that everyone's experience is unique; despite this, there are common narrative themes that the countless variations express. One of these is alienation—depression as feeling alone and cut off from God, oneself, other people, and meaningful things of value. A logical extreme of the alienation-from-value theme is nihilism, a philosophical narrative about life being meaningless: "The universe we observe has precisely the properties we should expect if there is, at bottom, no design, no purpose, no evil and no good, nothing but blind, pitiless indifference."[7] Here is a related observation from Francesca:

> Once I believe what he thought of me I feel really small, like I'm someone who can be hurt without a care, so unimportant that he could just be dissecting a dead frog, or kicking a stone. My father believed that I as a person was just nothing, and one of my counselors, when I was thinking of giving up on seeing her, reminded me about this. She said my thinking about quitting was "nihilism," and she was on target—the reason I didn't want to even try any more to change was I thought that it is all a bullshit waste of time. Being told this about my nihilism was a shock to me, since I'd never seen myself as that way. But there is that streak, and it used to be very strong.

A powerful aspect of alienation from oneself is being estranged from one's feelings, distancing oneself from anger,[8] sadness, and other "negative" emotions and also numbing in relation to all affect, including pleasurable feelings—love, gratitude, self-worth, and happiness are examples.

Along with alienation from God and oneself, it's not uncommon for a depressed person to be alienated from other people, even people who have been important sources of love and support in

7. Dawkins, *River out of Eden*, 133, quoted in Clayton, *Religion and Science*, 26. Nihilism is an extreme logical extension of reductionism, a "this and nothing more" propensity in explaining the causes or meaning of things.

8. Arieti and Bemporad, *Severe and Mild Depression*, 176–81; Birnbaum, *Cry Anger* was a popular classic.

happier times. This is understandable—the same sense of very low self-worth and experience of the world in general being without value can easily be extended to other people. Perhaps feeling dismissed or diminished by their friend, it would be unsurprising for them to withdraw, and a vicious circle developing. Feeling alone and alienated, Francesca could withdraw from the very people she would otherwise have relied on for love and support. "Part of me is still surprised," she writes, "that I have any friends and that Sandy [her partner] has hung in with me. They tell me I could be hard to put up with when I was off in my own miserable world—they just figured I would snap out of it and I guess at times I did. I was never a total loner. Thank God for people giving me second chances."

Social Isolation and Resources

With examples like Francesca before us receiving much attention, it is easy to assume that depression is normally caused by negative childhood experiences. While this is common enough, as we noted above it is also the case that people can be depressed because of lifestyle issues, deprivation, and/or oppression in their current life circumstances. If someone is struggling with addiction, poverty, violence in her or his relationships, or abusive treatment at work, for example, such issues can be a priority focus for alleviating depression. Other examples are things like unemployment, inequality, prejudice, war, chronic fear, one's children or other family members suffering, and injustice.

The social supports and resources we all need if we are to flourish have been discussed using four categories:[9] concrete and instrumental resources, informational/educational resources, emotional supports and access to meaningful social roles.

9. Cameron, "Potential of Informal Support Strategies in Child Welfare"; Rothery, "Family Therapy with Multiproblem Families"; see also Hodge, *Spiritual Assessment in Social Work and Mental Health Practice* for depth and detail about social connectedness and mental health issues. For a more theoretical overview of this general topic area see Rothery, "Critical Ecological Systems Theory."

1. Concrete and instrumental resources include all the basics; in Francesca's case she was financially secure, so food and lodging were not an issue. As we know, she had a need for addiction and mental health services, which she had made extensive use of in the course of her life—she lived in an urban setting where a range of such services was available at a manageable cost.

2. Informational/educational resources include access to the knowledge and skills one needs to flourish. Francesca, for example, had a need for information regarding addictions, depression, and childhood sexual abuse survival. Over some years, she accessed counseling and programs that had educational components, and her journal demonstrated that she became very knowledgeable about the issues with which she struggled and about the psychotherapeutic arts/ sciences in general.

3. Emotional supports come to us through relationships in which we can discuss our vulnerabilities knowing it is safe to do so and that we will be well understood. Francesca relied on her relationship to Sandy in this regard, and she also utilized professional help that was supportive in this way. Further, she saw her church as being a source of a couple of relationships that she found emotionally supportive, especially one with another sexual abuse survivor. Her relationship with her mother was somewhat distant and is not frequently discussed in her journal.

4. Access to meaningful social roles comes through work or other activities in which we feel welcome and think our competence is recognized. In her earlier years, especially when she was actively alcoholic, Francesca had a problematic work record. Part of the counseling she received over time focused on career planning after she quit drinking; eventually she was able to establish herself in a job in a social service agency, as an administrative support person. Her intelligence and genuine interest in people (and also a strong work ethic)

contributed to her becoming, relatively quickly, a valued employee in a sufficiently well-structured job she thought was worthwhile. Not all working relationships in this large agency were positive, of course, but some were and served as sources of positive feedback for her.

When she was quite young, Francesca developed a passion for music, an interest that she credited, in her journal, with saving her life.[10] Her first love was for the clarinet and she switched as a teenager to the saxophone. She apparently became very competent musically, doing well in a university music program until dropping out in her final year (she attributed this to her drinking and depression).

Looking at these various types of resources sheds light on Francesca's resilience. Over time, she was able to access some of the key things she needed in order to flourish, and to make these resources an integrated part of her life. If her story had been more one of continued deprivation, it would likely have been less optimistic.

Reader Reflections

In a spirit of friendly curiosity, write or talk about any of the following reflections that look interesting to you:

1. Think about your own life and the resources you have access to at this point. Note deficiencies you would like to remedy and, if appropriate, identify anyone who you could ask for help with figuring out how to proceed:

   * Concrete resources like food, lodging, or medical care;

   * Informational/educational resources—anything it would be good for you to learn more about;

   * Emotional resources—someone to talk to who can respect the things you feel vulnerable about;

---

10. It is not uncommon for depressed and/or traumatized people to credit the creative arts with life-saving properties: see, for a rather stark example, Rhodes, *Instrumental*; see also Styron, *Darkness Visible*, 65–67.

* Access to meaningful social roles—things you do where you feel welcome and competent.

2. Without intending to actually mail it, write Francesca a letter telling her how her journal is serving as a resource to you in your own journey.

3. Which of depression's many roots or causes have you habitually regarded as most important? What does this imply about what kind of help you usually think will be most effective?

4. If you think about the different people who can help when someone is feeling depressed, who comes to your mind first? Last? What are your reasons for these choices?

5. How would you answer the five narrative questions with respect to yourself at this point? It's a good idea to keep your answers brief if you can. Some of your answers may come as a surprise, even to you yourself—identify these as something you may wish to explore further.

* What sort of person am I?

* What is this world like?

* What can I expect from other people?

* What can I expect from God?

* What does a person like me do with her or his life, in a world like this, in the company of people like these, with the nature of God being what it is?

4

Sin, Repentance, and Forgiveness

If we say that we have no sin, we deceive ourselves,
and the truth is not in us.[1]

It [the Bible] is unequivocal about the fact that something has gone wrong.[2]

Sin

IN CONVERSATIONS BETWEEN CHRISTIANS and atheist or agnostic secular humanists, the term *sin* can be decidedly awkward. It is a word that is seldom or even never used in polite secular society, while for Christians it tends to be critically important: "Christ died for our sins" they say, and that puts the concept of sin at the center of their worldview. "The language of sin (and forgiveness) dominates the Christian imagination."[3]

A common definition holds that sin is simply rebellion against God, motivated by pride. Another emphasizes violence against God's creation.[4] For our purposes, and using language consistent

1. 1 John 1:8.
2. Borg, *Heart of Christianity*, 165.
3. Borg, *Heart of Christianity*, 164.
4. Suchocki, *Fall to Violence*, 12; see also Borg, *Heart of Christianity*, 166.

with that introduced earlier in this book, *sin is alienation from God by engaging in processes that mitigate against flourishing.* It's another very important fuzzy concept.

Borg implies that the idea of sin may have become *too* fuzzy, an overly broad metaphor for everything that can go wrong in our lives, which could be usefully replaced by a more differentiated set of concepts:

> Imagine the difference it would make if Christian worship services also highlighted the other biblical images [in addition to sin] for what ails us. Imagine Christian liturgies and preaching that emphasize that we are Pharaoh's slaves in Egypt and need liberation, that we are exiled in Babylon and need a path to return home, that we are blind and need to see again, that we are sick and wounded and need healing and wholeness.[5]

So, things can go wrong that are not our doing, with respect to which feelings of guilt, shame, and culpability are not appropriate. Indeed, baseless and misplaced feelings of guilt and shame are often one of depression's roots and are a counterproductive hindrance in the search for relief. For example, we have noted that like many abuse survivors Francesca has irrationally felt responsible for and guilty about her victimization at the hands of her father.

A more general point is that we may become unhealthily preoccupied with sin, as if it was the most important feature, to the exclusion of very significant others, of our lives as Christians: "For the most part where the Church has erred is in stressing humanity's propensity to sin at the expense of our equally real capacity to care about justice,"[6] not to mention our creative capacities devoted to love, truth, beauty. and morally correct choices.

---

5. Borg, *Speaking Christian*, 151.

6. Harries, *Beauty and the Horror*, Kindle loc. 3447; see also Borg, *Speaking Christian*.

Repentance

Francesca writes:

> I was reading Peck's book[7] where he mentions how "facing the music" is such an interesting expression. I told [names counselor] about this and she said she thought it's all about repentance. I thought that's smart, and I told her my personal #1 example of repentance was when I quit drinking. It wasn't easy facing *that* music!

"Facing the music," like "repentance," connotes confronting sin and making corrective changes; often this means stepping onto a new path, described as turning or returning back to God. The fit for Francesca was perfect, since for her quitting drinking preceded a spiritual reckoning involving a return to attending church. In part she attributed this transformation to the twelve-step program she participated in to achieve her sober lifestyle—the program emphasized involvement of a power greater than herself to assist in her struggle. "I was embarrassed by that at first," she writes, "but now I think it was one of the most important things AA did."

Forgiveness

Citing Griswold, Martha Nussbaum offers a "working account" of what is meant by forgiveness: "Forgiveness . . . [is] a two-person process involving a moderation of anger and a cessation of projects of revenge, in response to the fulfillment of six conditions:

1. Acknowledge that she was the responsible agent
2. Repudiate her deeds (by acknowledging their wrongness) and herself as their author
3. Express regret to the injured at having caused this particular injury to her
4. Commit to becoming the sort of person who does not inflict injury and show this commitment through deeds as well as words

---

7. Likely Peck, *Road Less Travelled.*

5. Show that she understands, from the injured person's perspective, the damage done by the injury . . .

6. Offer a narrative accounting for how she came to do wrong, how that wrongdoing does not express the totality of her person, and how she is becoming worthy of approbation.[8]

In Griswold's full account of this "surprisingly complex and elusive notion,"[9] there are more criteria yet,[10] and examples of complete or pure forgiveness must consequently recede from view as something that is rarely if ever observed in the real world. The criteria are useful indicators regarding what may be observed or expected in different cases, but (as Griswold himself recognizes) the difficulty that would arise using them all as criteria to be met is obvious. For one thing, if one thinks about Francesca and her father, one is inclined to object that a *two-person process* is neither desired nor advisable. At the same time, there are things Francesca might do about putting her past abuse in its place (i.e., it is *past*). We might want to acknowledge these as a kind of forgiveness appropriate to her unique circumstances and needs. We will discuss this point further in chapter 6, on trauma.

Nussbaum has a further helpful elaboration:

> Some less codified parts of the Jewish tradition and some well-known parts of the Christian tradition also introduce two different attitudes. One I shall call *unconditional forgiveness;* the other I shall call *unconditional love and generosity.* . . . These alternatives have a great deal to offer. And both are prominent in biblical texts, in both the Old and New Testaments.[11]

Of these two "attitudes," unconditional forgiveness has most to do with our present purposes. It refers to the not-uncommon situation where there is "a moderation of anger and a cessation of

---

8. Nussbaum, *Anger and Forgiveness*, 57; also Griswold, *Forgiveness*, 149–50; see also Griswold, xvi regarding the two-person criterion.

9. Griswold, *Forgiveness*, xiv.

10. Nussbaum, *Anger and Forgiveness*, 272.

11. Nussbaum, *Anger and Forgiveness*, 60.

projects of revenge" with no expectation of preconditions being met. The process is wholly implemented by the forgiver, independent of any input from the forgiven. Years after her father's death, Francesca reported that her feelings of anger toward him had abated somewhat, along with some consideration on her part of what the reasons for his abuse might have been. "I will never love him," she wrote at this point in her life, "but I don't put as much time and energy into feeling angry, and I like having more control over that. I even wonder sometimes what it was that caused him to be who he was."

As is very often the case, Francesca also felt guilty and ashamed about having been an alcoholic, and there is a somewhat paradoxical aspect to her wish for forgiveness from people she felt guilty toward. On one hand she felt she had not been in control of her addiction, and yet she still accepted a degree of responsibility for things she had done while under the influence. Driving while inebriated was a prominent example for her:

> I have asked God for . . . forgiveness for my drunk driving. I can say I was powerless, and that seems true, there is something to that, but God also knows I knew . . . I was seriously over the line. Not only that but I did finally quit, so I had some choice about my drinking.
> My addiction was not really my fault. What I had to deal with was too much for a lonely little girl to handle. But . . . God knows I was making choices and I do have some guilt. If I had killed somebody with my car, I would have been the responsible party. I could have been jailed. I bet *that* would have led me to quit drinking sooner instead of later.

Perhaps Francesca simply must reconcile herself to a burden of guilt that troubles her on a long-term basis (she is not alone; most people harbor regrets). Her understanding of Scripture is that she should still get on with her life—in this respect she copied John 8:3–11[12] into her journal:

---

12. King James Version.

And the scribes and Pharisees brought unto him a woman taken in adultery; and when they had set her in the midst, they said unto him, Master, this woman was taken in adultery, in the very act. Now Moses in the law commanded us, that such should be stoned: but what sayest thou? This they said, tempting him, that they might have to accuse him. But Jesus stooped down, and with his finger wrote on the ground, as though he heard them not. So when they continued asking him, he lifted up himself, and said unto them, He that is without sin among you, let him first cast a stone at her. And again he stooped down, and wrote on the ground. And they which heard it, being convicted by their own conscience, went out one by one, beginning at the eldest, even unto the last: and Jesus was left alone, and the woman standing in the midst. When Jesus had lifted up himself, and saw none but the woman, he said unto her, Woman, where are thine accusers? hath no man condemned thee? She said, No man, Lord. And Jesus said unto her, Neither do I condemn thee: go, sin no more.

It is useful to revisit the circle of compassion metaphor[13] at this point. The "scribes and Pharisees" invoke Mosaic laws in order to define the adulterous woman as being outside the circle and as therefore not deserving of compassionate treatment. Consequently, she would be a candidate for execution by stoning. Jesus challenges their definition of her when he intervenes by reminding the accusers that they too have committed sins; if they are eligible for compassion despite that, then so is she. She is thereby forgiven, moved back within the circle where she is seen to deserve the protections that compassion affords.

On Forgiving Oneself

Griswold prefers to think about forgiveness as involving two (perhaps more) people, so he is understandably nervous about the notion that one can forgive oneself: "Self-forgiveness is rightly suspected of abuse. The spectacle of preachers of the faith caught

13. See page 5.

in flagrante and forgiving themselves with lightening speed naturally feeds cynicism about the whole concept."[14] However, there is a contrary argument that is very important in managing depression. We would note that people are complex, multifaceted, and fully capable of self-reflection. If Francesca can hold herself responsible for wrongs she committed while drunk, she can also be self-forgiving, leaving aside the question of if and when being so is morally defensible. For depressed people, self-castigation is very commonly a problematic aspect of their narrative—Francesca, we have noted, at one time wished that she was someone else: "Anybody but me, any place but this, any time but now" was a repeated refrain in her journal. As with most depressed people, self-love was for her a deeply important but elusive narrative accomplishment, and one that depended on a prior willingness to forgive herself. Whereas she once blamed herself for her abuse, she was eventually able to write, "I am a survivor, and I'm surprised to see how tough and brave I was when I was still just a kid. It's not exaggerating to say that without that I'd be dead."

Like everyone, Francesca can observe herself and talks to and about herself. She stands at the center of a narrative of which she is also the author. Seeing herself as a survivor rather than as a culpable victim is a vital act of authorial self-forgiveness. She is able, as prescribed by playwright Arthur Miller in *After the Fall*,[15] to take her life into her own arms, to move herself decisively to a position within her own circle of compassion.

Reader Reflections

In a spirit of friendly curiosity, discuss or write about any of the following reflections that look interesting to you:

1. Discuss or write about one of your own experiences with repenting, finding a new path after realizing something was wrong.

14. Griswold, *Forgiveness*, 122.
15. Miller, *After the Fall*, Kindle loc. 506.

2. Do you have a personal example of something you feel guilty or ashamed about that is or was not your responsibility?

3. Have you ever felt pressure to forgive somebody for something when you sensed it was not (at least at that point) something it would be good for you to do?

4. Do you have an example of when you forgave somebody for something and felt good about it afterward?

5. Do you have an example of a time when you yourself were forgiven for something and felt good about it afterward?

5

NARRATIVES ABOUT PERFECTIONISM
Guilt, Shame, and Redemption

Be perfect, therefore, as your heavenly Father is perfect.[1]

I thought if I could just be good enough the abuse would stop.[2]

Knowledge is important, but only if we're being kind and gentle with ourselves as we work to discover who we are.[3]

PERFECTIONISM CAN BE A relatively benign insistence on very high standards, but it can also be a toxic contributor to depression. The toxic case is not uncommon, and it is what we refer to throughout this chapter. Benign perfectionism is recognized and appreciated, but it is not our concern in what follows.

---

1. Jesus in Matthew 5:48.
2. Francesca's Journal.
3. Brown, *Gifts of Imperfection*, xi.

The Perfectionist's Narrative

The perfectionist's story consists in part of episodes that begin with a specific type of goal—a *dominant goal*.[4] An important aspect of this goal is that it is unachievable because the unspoken standard attached to it is fuzzy and impossibly high. Most of us read Francesca's wish to be a good enough girl that her abuse would stop understanding immediately that this is an impossible goal, a standard never to be reached; being *good enough* is by definition unattainable.

A close relative to the dominant goal is the *dominant other*, an exceptional person[5] by whom the impossible standard to be met is symbolized. This person represents standards of being that are both fuzzy and beyond the reach of all the rest of us. It is one thing to want to be a good Christian and another to insist one must be like Jesus in all respects. The first expectation is achievable while the second is maddeningly elusive.

Dominant goals and others are never in short supply, the availability of cultural icons being impressive. The world of sports has its superheroes and there are stars of stage and screen whose virtuosity has us shaking our heads in admiration. Being a musician, Francesca was guaranteed a supply of prodigies against whom she could compare herself and find herself wanting. In classical music there are historical figures like Bach and Mozart who are seen to be almost godlike, and more popular music has exemplars who inspire worshipful admiration from fans—being a saxophonist, Francesca could treat a few jazz giants as dominant others:

> On good days I could listen to [John] Coltrane or Lester Young and feel happy and excited about what they can do. Some other days, though, I got more depressed, thinking about how no matter how hard I practice I can

4. Arieti and Bemporad, *Severe and Mild Depression*, 141.

5. Arieti and Bemporad, *Severe and Mild Depression*, 140. We are defining the "dominant other" here slightly differently from the main focus and examples presented by Arieti and Bemporad, in ways consistent with what we know to be the experience of many depressed people, especially Christians, for whom Jesus represents an unattainable standard of being.

never do half of what they do just getting warmed up. My own music seemed useless next to them—I was just wasting my time trying.

Francesca is referring to a pattern consisting of just a few steps that can be remarkably predictable in the perfectionist's life. First there is a commitment to the dominant goal (or the dominant other's example), and then there is a period of striving to attain the impossible. Eventually it becomes clear the standard is not going to be *satisfactorily* met, and then there is a time of despair, the bitter taste of defeat. The pursuit of excellence ends in depression.

There are infinite variations to this common narrative, of course, human creativity being unfailingly impressive. It explains why some people report depressed feelings at times that should be cause for celebration. A young woman earns her medical degree and is moved to tears in the weeks following her graduation. Hoping to cure everyone in need, she finds it difficult to confront the limitations of real life as a doctor. Her unspoken goal was to save humanity, not merely to help some people to some extent some of the time.

Clearly, Christianity can be a perfectionistic doctrine—there is a lot of support for that in the life of Jesus and, as another example, the letters of Paul. There are saints like Mother Teresa, and martyrs like Martin Luther King Jr. Comparing ourselves to dominant others who are spiritual giants, we inevitably fall short, and the narrative consequences, the conviction that one has been proven worthless, can be awful to bear. Guilt-ridden, self-loathing Christians are the pitiable outcome when striving for excellence as a Christian turns toxic, when it becomes a series of perfectionistic episodes.

Sin and Redemption

To be born human is to be born as a flawed person in a flawed world. Since the beginning of our species, there has been something wrong; this is simply an existential fact of life. In her journal, Francesca coined the term "muckupedness," which admirably captures this reality. There is a propensity to sin that is human nature—something wrong that is part of every person's reality, and always will be.[6]

What we do as moral agents is strive to improve, as individuals, families, communities, and as whole cultures. We do our striving in a context that permits progress, but in which complete, ultimate success defies our expectations. So, we also ask for forgiveness and believe that it is freely given, God being a loving realist. This is redemption, and it is as much part of our ongoing reality as is sinfulness.

While Jesus allegedly instructs us to strive for perfection, he is also practical in his expectations of people in the real world. Consider Francesca's example in the previous chapter: Invited to participate in the legally sanctioned execution by stoning of an adulterous woman, Jesus tells her accusers that the first stone should be thrown by somebody who is perfect, who is "without sin." Sin being ubiquitous, there is nobody in the group who can make such a preposterous claim. The would-be executioners disperse, and Jesus tells the woman he does not condemn her, and that she should "go your way and . . . do not sin again" (John 8:11). She receives redemption and is to get on with her life. The same Jesus who is quoted as instructing us to be "perfect" is far from rigid and punitive in his reaction when someone falls short of the mark.

According to Yinger:

> The greatest problem in writing a book about perfection in biblical and theological tradition is the need to use the English word "perfect." . . . The Bible nowhere uses "perfect" in the sense we English-speakers normally assume (flawless conformity to a norm, sinless). It nowhere advances the notion that such flawless obedience is expected or required of human beings at any time.[7]

---

6. Harries, *Beauty and the Horror*, ch. 10.

7. Yinger, *God and Human Wholeness*, 1–2.

Acceptance

Acceptance, a redemptive antidote to perfectionism, is sometimes confused with passivity. This is a mistake:

> Acceptance . . . is the opposite of resignation and defeat. The Archbishop and the Dalai Lama are two of the most tireless activists for creating a better world for all of its inhabitants, but their activism comes from a deep acceptance of what is. The Archbishop did not accept the inevitability of apartheid, but he did accept its reality.[8]
>
> The kind of acceptance that the Dalai Lama and the Archbishop were advocating is not passive. It is powerful. It does not deny the importance of taking life seriously and working hard to change what needs changing, to redeem what needs redemption.[9]

Acceptance of one's personal limitations is humility, which entails reality testing regarding self (and others) and promotes equity in relationships. Again, we emphasize that there is no problem with having high standards, as long as there is no unspoken certainty that one will fail and, having failed, be proven worthless. Indeed, acceptance includes the acceptance of inevitable mistakes and failures—people who achieve excellence in their lives commonly acknowledge that the ability to accept such missteps and setbacks is a necessary part of their recipe for success.

Perfectionism and Self-Forgiveness

Acceptance is also a precursor to forgiveness: "When we accept the present, we can forgive and release the desire for a different past"[10]—a powerful move mitigating the effects of perfectionism.

To underline again an essential point emphasized earlier in chapter 4, forgiveness is a very complicated issue. We should resist the common temptation to be simplistic about it. Though it is

8. Dalai Lama, Tutu, and Abrams, *Book of Joy*, 223–24.

9. Dalai Lama, Tutu, and Abrams, *Book of Joy*, 226.

10. Dalai Lama, Tutu, and Abrams, *Book of Joy*, 228.

controversial, we also argued in chapter 4 for the validity of *self-*forgiveness when one has fallen short by making mistakes. Whatever childlike transgressions Francesca had committed, forgiving herself was crucial, involving recognition that her being imperfectly good had nothing to do with her father sexually abusing her:

> If I wanted I could write down hundreds of things I did wrong, breaking a dish, coming home a little bit late from school on band practice day or after a music lesson, losing my purse at the mall—stuff like that. Part of me knew this was normal stuff that kids all do, but I was also sure the reason I was abused was in some way my mistakes. I just wasn't good enough. . . . Seeing it wasn't my fault was really hard and I needed lots of help with it even after I was in university and my father was dead. One of the first things I wrote in my journal was about me not being so bad as a kid.

Perfectionism and Narratives about Oneself

In chapter 2, we listed five basic questions that are important to everyone regarding authoring a life story: What sort of kid am I? What is this world like? What can I expect from other people? What can I expect from God? What does a kid like me do with her or his life, in a world like this, in the company of people like these, with the nature of God being what it is?

What sort of kid did Francesca consider herself to be? A belief that made her life chronically difficult was that she could do nothing right, and even ordinary mistakes were evidence regarding her flawed nature; she was globally incompetent, therefore unwanted and worthless.

What did she conclude early in her life regarding what the world is like? Above all else, it seems, she considered the world to be a dangerous place where even small, ordinary mistakes can have catastrophic consequences.

What can she expect from other people? On this point her narrative was complicated: she thought other people inflicted pain or were powerless to protect her; she also thought other people were constantly judging her, and finding her to be deeply disappointing and *bad*. Just as she felt judged, she judged others, and could idealize those of whom she approved while strongly denigrating others for being less than perfect (treating them the same way she saw herself being treated).

What can she expect from God? Again, there were complexities, even contradictions, with anger over feeling abandoned coexisting with a deep yearning for salvation, and for a connection to the Divine.

Given all we have just summarily noted, what does she decide to do with her life? Once more her narrative is complicated, with periodic strivings for exceptional accomplishments mixed with the conviction that her ultimate fate is to fail, through alcoholism and/or her chronic mood disorder.

Narrative Options

Francesca's resilience has to do in part with the fact that there was good news in her life, positive experiences that she recognized and drew upon, and that served as antidotes to her toxic perfectionism. Her love of music was vital to her success—it is true, for example, that jazz saxophonists like John Coltrane could be dominant others in perfectionistic episodes, but their work (and that of a select few other master musicians) also touched and inspired her. On the recommendation of one of her therapists she wrote John Coltrane a letter of appreciation, which she never mailed but did copy into her journal. She also wrote about a music teacher in her high school who reached out to her:

> Ms. Henderson knew I was mucked up due to problems at home. She got to know me over my four years at my high school and she figured out things were not ok between me and my father. She talked me into signing up for band when I was in grade nine, and she let me use the music room to practice in at lunch time. A couple of other kids started bringing their lunch to the music

room too and for a while we played together as a combo.
. . . Ms. Henderson brought in some music she thought
we would like, and sometimes she played too, on the
piano, I remember one book of songs from West Side
Story. She's another one [names counselor] had me write
a letter to, after one of our sessions.

Arts like music are similar to sports in that they can connect
with someone's perfectionism in detrimental ways. There is always
room for improvement and there are always potential dominant
others in comparison to whom one can feel like a failure. There were
enough rewards from music that Francesca stuck with it despite
periodic bouts of depressive angst. In chapter 3, we discussed how
important it is for people to have access to social roles in which they
feel welcome and their competence is recognized, and we recounted
that Francesca credited music with having saved her life.

Perfectionism and Narratives about Change

Now there was a great wind, so strong that it was splitting
mountains and breaking rocks in pieces before the Lord,
but the Lord was not in the wind; and after the wind an
earthquake, but the Lord was not in the earthquake; and
after the earthquake a fire, but the Lord was not in the fire;
and after the fire a sound of sheer silence.[11] When Elijah
heard it, he wrapped his face in his mantle and went out
and stood at the entrance of the cave. Then there came a
voice to him that said, "What are you doing here, Elijah?"[12]

As we noted in chapter 3, in her journal Francesca recounted an
incident of abuse in which her father struck her forcefully enough
that she had to grab a railing to stop herself from falling down the
stairs to the basement of the family home:

11. In the King James Version the translation is "and after the fire a still
small voice."

12. Kings 19:11–14.

> I remember hanging on to the stair rail and thinking I
> should let myself fall. My thought was that if I broke my
> arm and somebody figured out I'd been hit, that might
> be enough to change things somehow. I wasn't really
> clear about this and anyway I didn't let go of the railing.
> I hung on. I'm still not one to let go. . . . People at church
> sometimes talk about the need to take a leap of faith, but
> I'd rather take one step at a time. This is my instinct, and
> I agree with the counselor who told me to listen to the
> voice telling me to hang on until it's safe to move. It's ok
> to take time.

We are a culture that values decisiveness and quick, definitive
actions, and we tend to think important changes come quickly at
moments of truth, choice, and determination. Similarly, the leap of
faith is a defining moment in many accounts of spiritual journeys.
Paul's revelation on the road to Damascus, for example, doesn't
seem to have involved any dithering on his part.

Moments of truth in which change happens are real enough,
but they are seldom the whole story. Francesca's experience with
quitting drinking is a common example:

> I have been sober for a few years now, but still don't
> understand exactly how I quit. Like most alcoholics,
> I struggled, deciding to quit dozens of times but never
> succeeding for more than a few hours or a day. Once, I
> went three weeks without a drink before I caved. It felt
> like coming home, and I figured I was a hopeless case.
> Finally, after a really bad week I checked myself in for
> treatment, and it just stuck. I remember passing the three
> week mark and wondering if I was really going the dis-
> tance. I offered to take my counselor out for a beer to
> celebrate, a little joke that didn't go over too well.

Women leaving abusive relationships may report breaking
them off more than once before achieving a lasting separation,
and many people who wrestle with weight control have a catalog
of diets they have tried with, at best, some temporary successes.

Addictions, weight control, bad relationships—people can
and do deal successfully with these and other problems. Perhaps

the simple point is that such changes are usually a process rather than a one-off event, and we should not feel defeated if we have to make more than one decision on the way to important goals.

So too with spiritual growth: Elijah, looking for something dramatic, has to fail to find God in the mother of all windstorms, in an earthquake, and in a fire before he finally hears the silence, the still, small voice inquiring gently what he is up to. In Francesca's account:

> I've sometimes felt like a second-rater spiritually, because my born-again friends had stories about powerful experiences of finding Jesus. Looking back, I suppose I could say I've been born again, at least that I'm a different, better person because of my faith. But I've never felt actually lifted up by God and never been touched by tongues of fire. It's been more of a step at a time journey in my case. As [names a counselor] told me often, it's ok to take time.

Goals: Beyond Happiness

Like many addicts, Francesca tried to manage her alcohol consumption on her own, by continuing to drink but attempting to moderate the amount. After several years of failing with this approach, and after a particularly bad binge, she signed on to Alcoholics Anonymous, a twelve-step program that had abstinence as its goal:

> For me, professional help and quitting altogether was the right path. Nothing else was going to work as far as I could see, and [names counselor] helped with a referral to a program. I stuck with it a day at a time and, with one relapse, I have stayed sober. Coming up to the twenty-year mark, I caught myself thinking about celebrating that accomplishment with a glass or two of wine. I could tell [names a different counselor] was worried about this and at her suggestion I went back and read what I wrote in my journal after my other relapse. This was surprisingly hard, but I did it and it worked, and I decided not to cave. Sandy was very relieved.

Even where there are no addictions issues, seeking help for depression can be or at least resemble an act of repentance—it involves facing up to something that is wrong and turning onto a new path. Importantly, even if the new path is not entirely depression free, there is much to be learned from following it.[13] Under such circumstances, Laird recommends forbearance and a disciplined self-awareness:

> While we clearly prefer to be relieved of this burden, sometimes this simply does not happen. If it seems that depression is a frequent pattern of our inner weather, semipermanently or for such very long stretches of time as to seem permanent, it is important for us to get to know our depression in intimate detail rather than futilely insist that it go away. . . . Even if depression does not loosen its grip, the skills of self-knowledge and inner vigilance remain life-giving.[14]
>
> Even as it resists treatment, depression can give birth to many beautiful children: deep insight into oneself as well as other people; profound compassion for all, especially the suffering; the ability to see straight through this uninvited guest who has moved in long enough to claim squatter's rights. Just like any affliction, depression can become a place of intercession and solidarity with others.[15]

Certainly, Francesca's depression had to some extent claimed "squatter's rights." She saw the need to manage her condition as a life-long reality, and was reconciled to that:

> The path I'm on is not what I expected at first. I still take antidepressant meds and check in with my counsellor. I sometimes feel nervous and afraid (panicky) for no reason that makes sense these days. Never mind, I still like the path I found and like who I am, and that's what matters. I'm surprised that there's nobody I would trade

13. See Laird, *Ocean of Light*; part 3 is titled "Our Uninvited Guests" and is a valuable extended discussion of situations like these.

14. Laird, *Ocean of Light*, 187.

15. Laird, *Ocean of Light*, 191–92.

places with. In spite of the problems, I hate what happened, but like my life. . . . I think of myself as a pilgrim.

Part of the discussion of depression in chapter 3 emphasized complexity—indeed, though there are common themes, no two people will experience depression in exactly the same way.[16] Because of our creativity, common themes have infinite variations.

To the complexity of depression add the complexity of flourishing, its antithesis, as described at the beginning of chapter 2. Positive emotions are but one of five elements comprising a state of well-being or flourishing[17] and an analysis of each of these elements makes the picture increasingly complicated. There are, for example, at least fifteen different positive feelings.[18] The beneficial outcomes that come with managing depression more effectively simply will not be the same for one person versus the next; indeed, they may also vary in the *same* person from time to time.

Francesca's depression was largely due to trauma, to childhood sexual abuse, and such a history presents particular challenges (see chapter 6):

> I still take two antidepressant meds, at a fairly high dose. I occasionally try cutting back on these, but my whole body reacts negatively, so I'm ok to live with it. I'm still sensitive to the way people treat me, especially men, and affectionate gestures can be triggers causing me to be afraid. Sandy and I understand this and know how to manage it, but not everyone understands and I'm sure I'm seen by some as unfriendly. On the other hand I'm content with my church life, my marriage, my work, my friendships, and my counselor. I've been learning about centering prayer and I'm keen about that. One step at a time. I used to say "anybody but me, any place but this, any time but now" but I've realized I don't want to be somebody other than me anymore.

16. See Solomon, *Noonday Demon*; and Styron, *Darkness Visible*.
17. Seligman, *Hope Circuit*.
18. Dalai Lama, Tutu, and Abrams, *Book of Joy*, 33–34.

Francesca was able, over time, to rewrite her story; rather than a hopeless victim, she defined herself as a competent survivor (much of the time). This did not happen overnight, and her changes were not single, one-off events. She did make many significant changes, of course, but there was no magic, and no single, blinding born-again experience that miraculously changed everything once and for all. In fact, accepting the step-by-step, relapse-ridden, occasionally messy reality of how change normally happens was itself a change she had to make.

In earlier days, Francesca could succumb to the belief that change had to be perfect. Anything less than that, she thought, was worthless, leaving her vulnerable and unsafe. With help, she developed a more accepting and forgiving narrative that valued steps in the right direction rather than imposing an all-or-nothing standard—"all," of course, being fuzzy and impossible.

For a considerable time, Francesca never reread earlier entries in her journal, and there are gaps of time when she wrote nothing at all despite the fact that she knew writing was useful. When she was harboring fantasies of "trying out" drinking again, her counselor advised her to revisit entries she had authored some years earlier in coming to terms with a relapse. This proved useful, and she agreed to follow it up by going back further in time, to when she had first stopped drinking successfully, with the support of an Alcoholics Anonymous type of program. She was very reluctant about following through on that advice, expecting it would result in shame and embarrassment over what she had written:

> I was so sure that what I'd written was mucked-up garbage that I often thought about just deleting it. I was sure it would be embarrassing and depressing to read it, and pointless. What I found when I did finally look at it was a surprise, I had written some really honest stuff about the trouble I was in and how I had sabotaged myself other times when I tried to quit. Just trying one drink was one of the thoughts I tempted myself with, and I was smart enough to know what I was up to, pretty well every day for months and months. . . . Thank God I didn't hit the

delete key but kept on reading instead. That mucked-up garbage has saved me from a lot of grief, I think.

Reader Reflections

In a spirit of friendly curiosity, discuss or write about any of the following reflections that look interesting to you:

1. Remember a time when you were acutely depressed and write that depressed self an imperfect letter. In that letter describe *one* of the things you hope to accomplish as you grow, *one* of the steps you can take and will consider successful.

2. Choose a mistake you feel badly about, even though it is in the past. Write about or discuss the desirability of you forgiving yourself for that mistake.

3. Choose a mistake you think someone you care about has made in relation to you. Discuss or write about the desirability of you forgiving that person for that mistake. There may be no perfect way to handle this—what would be a good enough step in the right direction?

4. Write Francesca a letter expressing compassion toward her and her earlier tendency to blame herself for her sexual abuse.

5. Write about or discuss a problem you had that you think you handled sufficiently well, without having solved it perfectly. Consider whether you think you should now leave that problem alone or should try to do more in a search for a better solution. Imagine a friend telling you about a similar situation. What would your advice be?

6

Trauma

Nothing in the future can justify what is happening now.[1]

Varieties of Traumatic Experience

Trauma is yet another critically useful but fuzzy concept. Some definitions emphasize *types* of events, stresses that can overwhelm people to the point where they can't effectively cope. The DSM-5, for example, focuses on events "that may cause or threaten death, serious injury, or sexual violence to an individual. a close family member, or a close friend."[2] With a different emphasis, the American Psychological Association considers trauma to be the *emotional effects* of debilitating stress rather than the stressful events themselves:

> Trauma is an emotional response to a terrible event like an accident, rape or natural disaster. Immediately after the event, shock and denial are typical. Longer term reactions include unpredictable emotions, flashbacks, strained relationships and even physical symptoms like

---

1. Harries, *Beauty and the Horror*, Kindle loc. 2918.

2. American Psychiatric Association, *Diagnostic and Statistical Manual of Mental Disorders*, 830.

headaches or nausea. While these feelings are normal, some people have difficulty moving on with their lives.[3]

Courtois and Ford identify a very broadly defined condition, *complex trauma*, which is far more inclusive than the narrowly defined "classic" PTSD conditions recognized in the DSM. Their catalogue of potential traumatic stressors is indeed lengthy and comprehensive:

> In addition to those classic criteria, complex traumatic stressors involve relational/familial and interpersonal forms of traumatization and exposure that are often chronic and include threats to the integrity of the self, to personal development, and to the ability to relate to others in healthy ways. They include abandonment, neglect, lack of protection, and emotional, verbal (including bullying), sexual, and physical abuse by primary caregivers or others of significance or loss of these primary attachment figures through illness, death, deployment, or displacement of some sort. Although these stressors more commonly occur during childhood and adolescence, some occur in adulthood in such forms as domestic violence, kidnapping, war, torture, genocide, human trafficking, and sexual or other forms of captivity or slavery. Additionally, complex trauma may be based on and associated with the victim's very identity, including such immutable characteristics as race, ethnicity, skin color, gender, genetic and medical conditions and physical limitations, family/tribal/clan background and history, and other factors, such as religious and political orientation, class, economic status, and resultant power or lack thereof (Kira et al., 2011). Traumatic victimizations based on these characteristics can literally begin pre-birth and be life-long or can occur primarily in adulthood.[4]

Attention to trauma as a mental health issue has waxed and waned for more than a century, the initial concern being soldiers

---

3. Quoted in Winnette and Baylin, *Working with Traumatic Memories to Heal Adults with Unresolved Childhood Trauma*, 52.

4. Courtois and Ford, *Treatment of Complex Trauma*, 9–10.

in times of war. Suffering from the debilitating symptoms of what is now commonly called post-traumatic stress disorder (PTSD),[5] people were sometimes provided humane medical attention, but they could also often be strongly stigmatized and relegated to positions outside the military's circle of compassion: "The soldier who developed a traumatic neurosis was at best a constitutionally inferior human being, at worst a malingerer and a coward. Medical writers of the period described these patients as 'moral invalids.'"[6]

Much important work has been accomplished, especially since the 1970s, clarifying what trauma is and what its implications are. Stigma remains, of course. There is no more talk of "moral invalids" though PTSD sufferers can still be treated as if they have character flaws. Where cults of masculinity remain influential, people who need sensitive, humane treatment can be dismissed as weaklings or malingerers. Still, growing numbers of traumatized people are demanding respectful attention. Increasingly, the voices of women are raised and heard (admittedly an uphill struggle), and the effects of child abuse and intimate partner violence are understood to be bona fide PTSD reactions, equal in severity and sharing definitive traits with the traumas associated with military service. As for prevalence: "Not until the women's liberation movement of the 1970s was it recognized that the most common post-traumatic disorders are those not of men in war but of women in civilian life."[7]

Another important accomplishment on the scientific front has been a greater understanding of the neurological effects of trauma, a subject that is outside the scope of this book, but which is noted because it is impacting the medical status and treatment of PTSD.[8]

5. Earlier labels for PTSD included "combat neurosis," "shell shock" and "battle fatigue".

6. Herman, *Trauma and Recovery*, 21. Similar dismissive characterizations can still be used in stigmatizing depression, as seen in chapter 1, where accusations of malingering are highlighted (see page 3).

7. Herman, *Trauma and Recovery*, 28.

8. See Van der Kolk, *Body Keeps the Score*, chs. 2–5.

Trauma and Depression

Francesca's depression was rooted in her sexual abuse history, and in this she's not alone. Not all depression is caused by trauma, but the frequency with which it *is* has been underestimated. Striking results from relatively recent research employing the Adverse Childhood Experiences Questionnaire (ACE) scale have shown this:

> The results were stunning: higher ACE scores were strongly correlated with greater incidence of the ten leading causes of death in the United States, including heart disease, lung disease, and liver disease. The intermediary factors were not hard to recognize: ACE scores were powerfully related to smoking, obesity, alcoholism, risky sexual behavior, and injection drug use. *ACE scores were also by far the most powerful predictors of clinical depression and suicidal behavior* [emphasis added]).[9]

The Problem of Evil

Unspeakably bad things happen to good people,[10] Francesca offering a clear case in point. Similar examples are not hard to come by, and therein lies a theological problem—the problem of evil, which has bedeviled theologians for centuries (see the book of Job in the Hebrew Bible). The problem of evil is the need to reconcile realities like Francesca's abuse with the belief that God is omnipotent and loving. Francesca felt angry with God for abandoning her in the most painful imaginable circumstances, a reaction that is shared by many survivors: "As survivors of childhood abuse, our anger toward God focuses around the issue of abandonment."[11] The pain is only heightened if it is also connected to feelings of profound guilt: "For the deeply religious, the conviction of inner badness that accompanies melancholia slides all too readily into a belief

---

9. Herman, *Trauma and* Recovery, 258; see also Chandon et al., "Mental Health Associated with Childhood Maltreatment."

10. Kushner, *When Bad Things Happen to Good People.*

11. Flaherty, *Woman, Why Do You Weep?*, 101.

that one has been cast out by God."[12] In any event, it is understandable when survivors demand answers to obvious questions: Where was God and why didn't s/he do something? However, when abuse is its source, anger is not straightforward and can be dysfunctional. "My anger wasn't good for anything," writes Francesca:

> Along with being mad, I wasn't able to do anything. I can agree with people who tell me my anger was understandable, except that it was also useless. When getting mad leads to something being done it can feel good, but for a long time it was just pointless because it didn't go anywhere. I just shut it off.

Thus, an important aspect of trauma is powerlessness; there is nothing one can do to contain the stress and pain. For this reason, to "just shut it off" may well be the only response available and coping with traumatic events often includes numbing all the feelings they evoke. Among the feelings that can be shut off are spiritual yearnings and anger. Accompanying the yearning and anger is a deeply demoralizing question: Why did God allow this to happen? This is the problem of evil: if God is omnipotent and loving, why is suffering apparently the lot of some good people, even the defenseless very young?

For some people the problem of evil leads to a rejection of God, though not for everyone.[13] Partly in response to Sandy's encouragement, Francesca was able to effectively sidestep the problem and allow a working relationship with God and a church community:

> Sandy admitted she didn't know why God couldn't help me but she was sure God hated my father's abuse, and never stopped loving me. This helped me move on, though I still get angry with God when I think about it. When I told Sandy this she laughed. "God can take it," she said.

---

12. Cregan, *Scar*, 36.

13. Frankl, *Man's Search for Ultimate Meaning*, 19, thinks the trauma of being incarcerated in concentration camps during the holocaust resulted in a loss of spiritual beliefs for some victims, while those beliefs were actually strengthened for others.

Some theologians believe that God does not intervene because s/he is able to influence people and events only through "liberating" power, but not the power to control and coerce:

> More important than the quantity of power attributed to God is the nature of God's power. When God's power is thought of in conventional terms as the ability to control others, the tendency is to affirm that kind of power at the human level as well. . . . There are, however, other ways of understanding "power." You may note that "power over" is not really creative. It controls some aspects of what has been created. But to bring into being well-informed, committed, sensitive people requires an entirely different kind of power, the kind of power that Abba[14] embodies. . . . Every event is the outcome of many factors, and . . . God is just one of these. This means that God never singlehandedly determines exactly what happens. We cannot read God's purposes off of history . . . God is always confronted by a world, which, to a very large extent, determines its own future. Attributing control to "God" has had terrible consequences.[15]

Trauma: The Narrative Challenge

Using our creative gifts, we develop a narrative about our lives that is, ideally, a varied and complex tapestry. Part of its strength and interest lies in the multitude of parts that comprise a whole person. Each of us occupies different roles, for example, and the parts that are in the foreground when we are parenting are not usually the parts that we enact at work, or when socializing with friends, or while praying at church. Ideally, we are comfortable with most of the parts we call "me," and the diversity of those parts makes for a rich autobiography.

14. *Abba* is Aramaic for "father," the word with which Jesus addresses God.

15. Cobb, *Jesus' Abba*, Kindle loc. 2106–23. See also Oord, *Uncontrolling Love of God*, and *God Can't*.

In chapter 4, we referenced a quote by one of playwright Arthur Miller's characters in *After the Fall*: "I think one must finally take one's life in one's arms."[16] If we are fortunate, we come to embrace our whole multitude. Normally we will welcome some parts more than others—there are parts of which we are not proud. Our story about ourselves is not an unblemished romance. Still, we embrace all of what constitutes *us*—ourselves—for better and for worse, even the parts we usually hide from friends and relatives.

Accomplishing a measure of self-acceptance can be a very elusive goal for people who have been traumatized:

> The sense of being inhabited by warring impulses or parts is common to all of us but particularly to traumatized people who had to resort to extreme measures in order to survive. Exploring—even befriending—those parts is an important component of healing.[17]

"Self-acceptance," says the impatient perfectionist, "Right! How long can *that* take?" The answer may be discouraging, but in truth it is not a short-term task and is not susceptible to quick problem-solving. A first obstacle is that the memories laid down in times of trauma are themselves imperfect. They are often not in narrative form, stories one can evaluate and rethink efficiently.[18] More often traumatic events are recalled as bits and pieces of experiences we'd rather not confront, as sounds or images or smells, or the tactile quality of a touch that was especially repulsive. What is more, these memories were stored along with the emotions the incidents provoked: fear and powerlessness. Francesca's account of effective help received is instructive:

> I went to [names therapist] for over four years, and I feel I owe her a lot. I remember she told me over and over that its ok to take one step at a time, that I shouldn't take a step until it felt safe enough. I trusted her. We started

---

16. Miller, *After the Fall*, Kindle loc. 506.

17. Van der Kolk, *Body Keeps the Score*, 278.

18. Van der Kolk and Fisler, *Dissociation and the Fragmentary Nature of Traumatic Memories*.

with the prickly feeling of his beard and his hot breath. It took some time to process that one.

I have a solid idea now of what he did to me, but it didn't start out like that.

Jayne McConnaughey's memoirs[19] tell a compelling story regarding trauma and *dissociation*, which is "the essence of trauma [in which the] . . . overwhelming experience is split off and fragmented, so that the emotions, sounds, images, thoughts, and physical sensations related to the trauma take on a life of their own."[20] In McConnaughey's case, entire parts or personalities had taken on a hidden life of their own—the task of identifying and befriending these "multiple personalities" was enormously challenging, painstaking work.

Bessel van der Kolk discusses the role of several different treatment modalities to help traumatized people come to terms with their experience, with general goals that are straightforward enough:

> A central task for recovery from trauma is to learn to live with the memories of the past without being overwhelmed by them in the present. . . .
>
> How well we get along with ourselves depends largely on our internal leadership skills—how well we listen to our different parts, make sure they feel taken care of, and keep them from sabotaging one another.[21]

In a similar vein, Judith Herman quotes one of her therapy group participants, "Lenore":

> The biggest things for me are the benefits of not keeping a secret and being able to talk about things that—I thought that if I ever talked about them I would melt and disappear into the ground, or people would go scurrying from the room like rats. And I found out that didn't happen, both for me and for other people. I can almost step outside myself now[22] and look at the circumstances,

19. McConnaughey, *Brave*, and *Jeannie's Brave Childhood*.
20. Van der Kolk, *Body Keeps the Score*, 66–67.
21. Van der Kolk, *Body Keeps the Score*, 279–80.
22. In days past psychoanalysts referred to this as the development of an

because I know how I would respond if someone told me my story. I would feel really sad for that person. So I hope I can keep that perspective.

In this brief statement [comments Herman] "Lenore" touches on many of the themes of this book: overcoming the barriers of shame and secrecy, making intolerable feelings bearable through connection with others, grieving the past, and coming to a new perspective with a more compassionate view of oneself in the present. Witnessing the lives transformed in this process of recovery is what enables us old-timers, the practitioners of "plain old therapy," to keep on keeping on.[23]

Trauma and Measured Forgiveness

When Jesus recommended to his disciples his Lord's Prayer, he emphasized forgiveness: "And forgive us our debts, as we also have forgiven our debtors"[24]—being forgiving is an attribute of God's and a virtue for her or his people to aspire to. Strong though this value is, not everything is forgivable,[25] and the Bible does not stipulate that one should forgive everything unconditionally and immediately upon request. Surely there are questions of timing, context, and the nature of the sin concerned.

Forgiveness is complicated, especially when sins like abuse are the focus. To begin with, it is a fuzzy concept and there are circumstances under which we should clarify what we mean when we invoke it. In chapter 4, we cited Griswold[26] and Nussbaum as offering a definition of forgiveness that is very stringent: "A two-person process involving a moderation of anger and a cessation of projects of revenge, in response to the fulfillment of six

---

"observing ego"; see Greenson, *Technique and Practice of Psychoanalysis*.

23. Herman, *Trauma and Recovery*, 276.

24. Matthew 6:12.

25. Matthew 12:32.

26. Griswold, *Forgiveness*, 149–50.

conditions"[27]—conditions that go at least partially unmet most of the time. When Francesca writes regarding her abusive father that "I will never love him, but I don't put as much time and energy into feeling angry . . . [and] I even wonder sometimes what it was that caused him to be who he was," she is taking a step that constitutes a very significant degree of forgiveness. Had her father still been alive, he might have asked for more, but it would be wrong to pressure Francesca to go further unless she wanted to and was appropriately self-protective in the process.

There is an alternative moral imperative that has considerable weight when forgiveness of abusiveness is considered, and that is accountability. If a forgiven perpetrator goes on to abuse the victim again, or traumatizes others, it is hard to claim a moral accomplishment has been achieved in that instance. Griswold's six conditions[28] are all about accountability and are potentially useful in such cases.

Spiritual and Religious Abuse

Like other forms of abuse, spiritual abuse is largely about control:

> Spiritual abuse happens when people use God, or their supposed relationship to God, to control your behavior for their benefit. The physical abuser might use their fist to threaten you. The verbal abuser uses their words. The spiritual abuser uses God (or the Bible, church, or religion) as their justification and/or threat.[29]

Although we are unaware of measures of the prevalence of abuse this broadly defined, it seems safe to say frequencies must be considerable. When the prevalence of much more narrowly defined abuses is measured, the findings are troubling. Citing O'Loughlin[30] and other sources, Tobin reports that known cases

27. Nussbaum, *Anger and Forgiveness*, 57.

28. See pages 33-4.

29. Diederich, *Broken Trust*, 54.

30. O'Loughlin, "Pennsylvania Report Documents over 1,000 Victims of

of sexual abuse by Roman Catholic clergy are disturbingly high: "These stories . . . [are] mounting evidence . . . of a global clergy sexual abuse epidemic within the Roman Catholic church."[31] Tobin also makes the important point that "spiritual violence is not unique to Christian or theistic faith communities . . . [and that] survivor testimony indicates . . . that clergy sexual abuse can also impact survivors' capacities for other, non-Christian or nontheistic forms of spiritual engagement."[32]

We have discussed how *alienation* is normally a fundamental part of a depressed person's experience, including alienation from oneself, from other people, and from things of value in God's creation. Alienation from God is a frequent consequence of spiritual and religious trauma, and of anger toward God for allowing various traumas (including childhood sexual abuse) to occur. Alienation from the church is also common, with the result that someone who has spiritual needs is cut off from any acceptable spiritual home or community—a potentially serious loss.

Sexually abused by her father rather than a cleric, Francesca nevertheless felt abandoned by and angry toward God for allowing her father to perpetrate against her. She credits Alcoholics Anonymous for helping her recognize the spiritual dimension to her distress and the potential role of God in her recovery. She credits her partner, Sandy, with facilitating her eventual return to church, which she found to be an important support and resource to her. Had her abuser been a cleric, it is easy to appreciate how much more difficult this important rapprochement could have been. Indeed, spiritual abuse can cause seemingly irreparable harm, with lasting damage to a victim's ability to enter into fresh relationships with religious faith leaders and church communities. Then, while spiritual needs remain part of the person's experience, the ability to meet those needs and to develop and grow spiritually is compromised.

Priest Abuse."

31. Tobin, "Religious Faith in the Unjust Meantime," 1.
32. Tobin, "Religious Faith in the Unjust Meantime," 5, fn. 4.

Reader Reflections

In a spirit of friendly curiosity, discuss or write about any of the following reflections that look interesting to you:

1. Consider a situation where a man has been abusive and requests his partner's forgiveness. In concrete terms, what might he mean—i.e., what might he be asking her or him to do or agree to?

2. If Francesca's father was still alive, what could it mean for her to forgive him? Of the possibilities, which ones seem to you to be or not to be good ideas?

3. Assuming everyone has experienced at least some trauma in her or his life, can you identify an experience that still causes you significant distress when you think about it?'

4. Do you have a close friend or loved one who has experienced significant trauma? How might this affect your relationship to that person?

5. Have you (or someone you know) ever experienced spiritual abuse? Briefly describe the event and its outcomes.

7

Spiritual Practices

The unexamined life is not worth living.[1]

The God Hypothesis

Of course, not everyone believes in or worships God.

A popular story has it that a great mathematician, Pierre Simon Laplace, presented Napoleon with a book he had written. After perusing it, Napoleon wanted to know if it was true that Laplace had entirely left God out of his important equations. Laplace replied that he had "had no need of that hypothesis."

It is often the case that people who are predominantly atheist or agnostic—secular humanists, for example—in dealing with depression make use of practices that are rooted in spiritual traditions. A prominent example of this is Buddhist mindfulness meditation, which has in recent years become an important tool for helping professions in the mental health field. As a treatment for depression, meditation has stirred up considerable interest; so popular is it that it is even the topic for a "Dummies" book.[2]

---

1. Socrates.
2. Gebka, *Managing Depression with Mindfulness for Dummies.*

Part of the discussion about the usefulness of mindfulness meditation in managing depression has been an explicit rejection of the God hypothesis. Belief in a deity is not, it is argued, essential to learning and using mindfulness techniques. These have been adopted by practitioners of cognitive behavioral therapy (CBT) as an essentially secular set of interventions,[3] and research has been accumulating regarding the positive contribution they make in that context. Heller[4] provides a useful catalogue of thirty-two meditation techniques with a secular humanist readership in mind. Hägglund[5] provides a general defense of the secular humanist "faith" as a complete philosophy of life.

Not everyone thinks that the God hypothesis has outlived its viability and importance, however, and it is not seen as necessarily a good idea to secularize practices that have spiritual origins. From her experience, Francesca reports that the God hypothesis was an important factor in her healing. Spiritual beliefs and practices were, she thought, a vital contribution to her resilience. Without them, she did not think she would have managed her alcoholism and depression as successfully as she did.

Other People and Solitude

There is a rhythm to our lives—we are engaged with others part of our time, while most everyone also needs time alone. Christ's work, healing and teaching, brought him into intense community with others, from which he withdrew at times to pray in solitude. Balancing time alone and time engaged with others is an important life skill.

Naturally, the balance we need to flourish varies from time to time, and from person to person. Someone who is temperamentally an introvert might find the presence of others eventually becomes stressful; strong introverts can easily overdose on even

---

3. For a rare exception, see Pearce, *Cognitive Behavioral Therapy for Christians with Depression*.

4. Heller, *Secular Meditation*.

5. Hägglund, *This Life*.

congenial company. In contrast, an extroverted person is energized by the presence of and recognition by others and might become bored or anxious when nobody else is about. Leaning one way or the other is not more or less virtuous, though we may be tempted to criticize people who are not like us as standoffish (introverts) or intrusive (extroverts). We call these "boundary issues," intending no compliment by that term when we use it.

When we worship, it is often in the company of other people, as well, we believe, as in the presence of God. Communal prayer is a staple religious observance for church-going Christians, and it serves important purposes. It keeps adherents connected to the unfolding drama that is the liturgical year from Advent and Christmas through Lent and Easter. The meanings of these times are deeply anchored for us through our joint celebration of them. Similarly, in many churches shared rituals are a necessary context for important sacraments, like the Eucharist, and for rites that mark our passages from birth to the grave.[6] Francesca comments on the importance of this:

> A couple that Sandy and I know adopted a baby and we went to his baptism. This was two or three weeks ago and ... I still feel good when I think about it. I've been really lonely for too much of my life [so] that just being part of something like that means an awful lot. John is a lucky little boy, and I hope people keep on getting together to cheer him on.

Corporate and Personal Prayer

At the same time as she was connecting to her church, praying with that community, Francesca felt the need to reflect personally on her spiritual experience, how it was unfolding, and what it meant to her. Gatta[7] argues that the prescribed liturgy of corporate prayers, important though it is, can become rote and stale. The

6. Gatta, *Life in Christ*.
7. Gatta, *Life in Christ*.

need is for a personal, reflective practice that complements our participation in communal practices.

Meditation and Contemplative Prayer

Practices rooted in spiritual disciplines have a technical, how-to-do-it aspect and a spiritual meaning aspect. As noted earlier, when a Buddhist practice, mindfulness meditation, was embraced by mental health professionals who found in it useful techniques for coping with depression, it was promoted as a secular humanist more than as a Buddhist skillset. More specifically, mindfulness techniques were added to practices associated with CBT, and developed within that secular humanist tradition. Research indicates that they are useful, especially for preventing recurrence, a common problem in the field.[8] Indeed, interest has mushroomed in mindfulness techniques as useful life skills, applicable far beyond the world of mental health professionals.

The ancient practice of contemplative prayer in the Christian traditions shares much with mindfulness at the level of technique, and detailed suggestions about practical procedures are available in its literature.[9] A difference between mindfulness-based CBT and Christian contemplative prayer is that the latter has not abandoned the God hypothesis. For books that emphasize more the spiritual meaning aspect of contemplative prayer or Christian meditation, see Martin Laird's and Jim Green's work.[10]

---

8. Segal et al., *Mindfulness-Based Cognitive Therapy for Depression*.

9. Finley, *Christian Meditation* offers a detailed, how-to-do-it guide to contemplative prayer. For practical techniques, see also Pearce, *Cognitive Behavioral Therapy for Christians with Depression*. As well, see Green, *Giving Up Without Giving Up*. People interested in Christian meditation should also visit the World Community for Christian Meditation at https://www.wccm.org, which has links to networking and learning opportunities.

10. Laird, *Ocean of Light*. Laird's book is invaluable, in part because it includes a chapter on managing depression. For its specific relevance to depression and Christian meditation, also see the book by Jim Green, referenced in the previous footnote.

Of course, we seek solitude but are never totally alone. Other people are with us in spirit, and we habitually engage in imagined conversations with people who are physically distant. And many of us believe God is always present to us and we find times when our sense of that presence abandons us to be painful.

Practice Options: Francesca's Journal

In chapter 4, discussing repentance, we included a journal entry by Francesca in which she acknowledges the importance of the spiritual aspect of AA for her recovery. She was, her journal reports, embarrassed by the idea of turning her life over to a higher power, but she persisted in the program and eventually admitted to how much that aspect of it had contributed to her success.

Francesca kept a journal for many years but did not visit it regularly until she quit drinking. Her journey subsequent to that decision was well documented in frequent journal entries. Throughout, she focused these entries on her addiction, and also on her chronic depression—her efforts to come to terms with that and manage it are a constant theme. In her mind these are very much interrelated issues, in any event, and she makes no effort to separate them one from the other. Nor does she separate her spiritual growth from her decision to quit drinking and manage her depression effectively. Her pathway to health is a spiritual path, and the focuses of her journal reflected that. Indeed, journal writing is itself a spiritual practice for Francesca, as it is for many people;[11] it is, in fact, a primary spiritual practice in her life.

An impressive feature of her journal is Francesca's honest self-reflection about difficult issues in her life, as in this example alluded to earlier in chapter 5:

> It's my anniversary—20 (count them: 20!!) years of sobriety. I celebrated by talking to [names counselor] about my thought that I might someday drink again. Maybe

11. Baldwin, *Life's Companion.*

on my 75th birthday I will toast myself with a glass of champagne. No harm in that, is there?

As I write this I pray that I won't fall for it. [Names counselor] was worried and thought I should go back in my journal and read what I wrote 20 years ago, when I walked into my first meeting.

Some things have changed, but not the sneakiness of my addiction. She's [her addiction] very good at what she does. Then again, I'm pretty good at managing her. I didn't really want to but did go back and read what I wrote then. . . . Imagine having to go through that stuff again. Yikes! Run away!

The woman [referring again to herself in the third person] who climbed on the wagon that day didn't like herself—she was clear about that. Quitting drinking opened a window on my life and I didn't like what I saw. In some ways I still don't. Guilt about my muckupedness still makes me disappointed in myself.

Best to decide I'm on the wagon for good. With God's help I will die sober.

That same self-reflective intelligence and honesty are brought to directly bear on her spiritual practices, on her praying:

As I tried to focus on the Jesus prayer[12] I couldn't concentrate. As usual, there was a feeling in my body of tension in the back of my head behind my eyes. If that feeling could talk it would say I was being stupid and lazy. I imagine I'm hearing my father's voice.

How does a stupid lazy person get over the feeling of being a hopeless case? A kid can be excused for giving up (which I never really did . . . something I easily forget).

12 Francesca is likely referring to a contemplative prayer in which the name of Jesus Christ and a request for his forgiveness and mercy are repeated, like a mantra.

Depression's Many Roots

When Francesca's talk with a concerned nurse (chapter 3) led to identifying depression as a serious concern, a consultation with a mental health professional was arranged. A psychiatrist thought she would be a candidate for antidepressant drug therapy but stipulated she would have to quit drinking. Francesca was frightened enough that she agreed to meet with a social worker, who referred her to an alcoholism rehabilitation program, which she attended on an inpatient basis for a time, with subsequent follow-up in her community. Part of her follow-up plan was to make full use of an Alcoholics Anonymous program and to consult with a therapist with special expertise in working with sexual abuse survivors.

By this time, her father was dead; her mother was supportive of her efforts to get her life back on track, helping cover the cost of treatment.

In consultation with a psychiatrist, a trial of antidepressant medications was initiated. In her journal, she described a lengthy process with an eventual prescription for two medications that, she agreed, were effective for keeping her depression under control.

Her journal's early pages focused a lot on the task of staying sober, and on the difficult process of coming to terms with her sexual abuse history. We have noted that part of her AA program included steps accepting the presence of and need for a "greater power" for support in arresting her addiction. Her journal entries about this were ambivalent at first, but she stayed with a program that involved prayer and an acknowledged reliance on God's support. Her trauma therapist was sensitive to her spiritual needs, and supported her in acknowledging her anger about God having abandoned her when she was most in need—a complex set of issues that received much attention in her journal.

Her partner was a member of a large urban church, and Francesca decided to join it as well. Her journal described a slow, one-step-at-a-time engagement with that spiritual community, which included accessing some of the resources it offered for spiritual seekers—such as a group that met weekly to discuss spiritual journal writing, and a three-day retreat on contemplative prayer that she and Sandy went to together. At one point she wrote about being interested in revisiting her love of music-making, but there is nothing indicating whether she followed that up or not.

What Francesca's story describes is, over time, a multifaceted approach in which she successfully addressed a number of resource needs relevant to her depression. Not everyone's package will be the same, obviously, but the general strategy is appropriate to many if not most people. Depression has multiple roots and Francesca's success was a matter of addressing (again, over time) a number of important needs: medical, psychotherapeutic, social, and spiritual. One practice that she maintained throughout was journal writing, another was medication, and a third was an ongoing arrangement for checking in, as needed, with a therapist she knew and trusted. Her need for emotional support was met by her psychotherapist, by one close friend at her church, and, most importantly, by her partner, Sandy. Also important was meeting her need for meaningful social roles, partly through her church affiliation and in part through a job she valued and was good at.

Spiritual Autobiography

Whether through writing or through conversation with others, a spiritual autobiography can be a powerful part of any person's reflective spiritual practices. It is not a matter of sitting down to write one's entire life story so much as the telling of particular critical incidents. Periodically, Francesca used her journal to explore events from her past that she knew were meaningful, events that had had an impact on her depression and/or her spiritual development. Some incidents were revisited several times, with interesting changes from one entry to the next.

Reader Reflections

In a spirit of friendly curiosity, discuss or write about any of the following reflections that look interesting to you:

1. In conversation or in writing, discuss an event that you identify as part of your spiritual autobiography. It is best to limit yourself to something that can be read or discussed in ten to fifteen minutes, understanding that you will likely want to do this exercise a number of times. The five narrative questions presented in chapter 2 may well serve as a useful framework for this exercise.

2. Identify some of the things you appreciate about your membership in any faith community you are a part of.

3. Discuss or write about what approach works best for you when you want to reflect on some aspect of your spiritual development and/or your experience with depression.

4. Discuss or write about how you would describe your temperament in terms of introversion and extroversion. How is this reflected in your spiritual practices?

5. Discuss or write about how you would describe your temperament in terms of introversion and extroversion, or any other terms you consider relevant. How is this reflected in your membership in any faith community you are a part of?

8

LOVE

God is love.[1]

It was unconditional love rather than controlling power that dominated Jesus' understanding of God.[2]

The first step to take is to become aware that love is an art, just as living is an art; if we want to learn how to love we must proceed in the same way we have to proceed if we want to learn any other art, say music, painting, carpentry, or the art of medicine or engineering.[3]

The "L" Word

ON A WHIM, WE randomly selected a dozen books from our professional libraries. These were books on family and marital development and therapy, child development, counseling, mental health and, more specifically, depression. We searched the tables of contents and indexes for the word "love" and found that it rarely occurs. It seems that "love" is not an important part of

1. 1 John 4:8.
2. Cobb, *Jesus' Abba*, Kindle loc. 320.
3. Fromm, *Art of Loving*, 4.

the vocabulary of the secular humanist helping professions—one suspects it is not a frequent topic for discussion in their meetings, or classrooms, or around their dinner tables. In contrast, novels, movies, television shows, and popular music are replete with stories of romantic love, and a search for *love* in an electronic version of the NSRV Bible yielded hundreds of hits. This entirely unscientific, quick-and-dirty research suggests that there is a lack of fit between the importance love is accorded by mental health professions compared to a significant part of their clientele.

In his first letter to the Corinthians, Paul is insistent about the critical importance of love for Christians, in what must be one of the most oft-quoted passages in the New Testament:

> If I speak in the tongues of mortals and of angels, but do not have love, I am a noisy gong or a clanging cymbal. And if I have prophetic powers, and understand all mysteries and all knowledge, and if I have all faith, so as to remove mountains, but do not have love, I am nothing. If I give away all my possessions, and if I hand over my body so that I may boast, but do not have love, I gain nothing. Love is patient; love is kind; love is not envious or boastful or arrogant or rude. It does not insist on its own way; it is not irritable or resentful; it does not rejoice in wrongdoing, but rejoices in the truth. It bears all things, believes all things, hopes all things, endures all things.
>
> Love never ends. But as for prophecies, they will come to an end; as for tongues, they will cease; as for knowledge, it will come to an end. For we know only in part, and we prophesy only in part; but when the complete comes, the partial will come to an end. When I was a child, I spoke like a child, I thought like a child, I reasoned like a child; when I became an adult, I put an end to childish ways. For now we see in a mirror, dimly, but then we will see face to face. Now I know only in part; then I will know fully, even as I have been fully known. And now faith, hope, and love abide, these three; and the greatest of these is love.[4]

4. 1 Corinthians 13:1–13.

Jesus is more succinct, but no less forceful, giving love an absolute prominence among Christians' moral obligations:

> "You shall love the Lord your God with all your heart, and with all your soul, and with all your mind." This is the greatest and first commandment. And a second is like it: "You shall love your neighbor as yourself." On these two commandments hang all the law and the prophets.[5]

In *The Art of Loving*, a classic in the psychoanalytic literature, we find this definition: "Love is the active concern for the life and the growth of that which we love."[6] Fromm is adamant that *love* must be seen as a verb rather than a noun, as a choice rather than something we fall into.[7] Drawing on Fromm and using terminology employed in this book, *love* can be defined as *an active commitment to the flourishing of another or oneself.* Fromm adds this: "Beyond the element of giving, the active character of love becomes evident in the fact that it always implies certain basic elements, common to all forms of love. These are *care, responsibility, respect* and *knowledge.*"[8]

Contemporary psychoanalytic thinking[9] would suggest that Fromm's definition (and ours) describes a mature love, a love understood as commitment to a long-term relationship in which the flourishing of another person is one's priority and project. An alternative is a more childlike, passionate attachment (naturally somewhat narcissistic, a characteristic we will return to shortly). The latter is often primarily what we mean when we talk about "falling in love" while the former, more mature option involves the work of relationship building and maintenance—less sexy, perhaps, but more enduring. Each form is valuable and adds zest to living, and each complements the other.

---

5. Matthew 22:37–40.

6. Fromm, *Art of Loving*, 21.

7. See also hooks, *All about Love*, 204.

8. Fromm, *Art of Loving*, 21.

9. Ayed, "'I Love You.'"

Love of Oneself

hooks[10] asserts that love for oneself is easy to talk about while it can be very elusive as an accomplishment. Francesca concurs:

> [Names counselor] makes a big deal of self esteem and I agree it is a big issue when I'm depressed. On bad days, I have written that I'd like to be anybody but me, and my hatred for myself was strong and it was definitely a problem. I have some admiration for myself at times now, and think I have been a strong survivor. But these feelings can be buried and hard to get to on bad days. [Names counselor] tells me I have to work on loving myself and she's right. But I don't always know how to do that. Sometimes it just seems impossible. Not hating myself is one thing, loving myself is another. Anyway, I don't ever wish I was someone else other than me these days and that's progress. I like that.

Most of us will applaud Francesca's steps toward self-acceptance and a greater affection for herself. She deserves to enjoy more self-love as part of her healing from childhood trauma. But we might also worry. At what point does self-love become a problem? When does it signify a lack of necessary humility? When do we consider that what we see is not healthy self-esteem but narcissism (to use the DSM-5 diagnosis)?

There are two considerations that help us decide when self-love may be problematic. If Francesca's narrative about herself paints herself idealistically—as somehow perfect and without flaws—then we might worry. Also, a love of self coupled with a lack of empathy for other people can mean that something important is missing from the picture. We are, after all, enjoined by Christ to love our neighbor *as we love ourselves*, not to love ourselves *instead of* the other people in our lives (or vice versa).

Neither of these indicators suggests concerns about Francesca—she is, if anything, too self-critical, and there's nothing to concern us about her ability to empathize with others. That said,

---

10. hooks, *All About Love*, 85.

depression normally involves a narrative in which feelings of worthlessness can predominate. A commitment to one's own flourishing (along with the flourishing of other people) is a goal in recovering from depression, not a problem to be zealously guarded against.

Love and Other People

Among a number of words describing different forms of love that we have inherited from classical Greek philosophers such as Plato and Aristotle is *eros*. *Eros* originally meant a passionate love of beauty; today "it is often referred to as a sexual desire, hence the modern notion of 'erotic.'"[11] Not uncommonly, sexual desire and pleasure are lost when one becomes depressed, and such a loss can be a side effect with antidepressant medications. Such was the case for Francesca (in relation to Sandy), which is not at all surprising, especially given her history of childhood sexual abuse:

> When we were talking about moving in together, I was hard to get along with sometimes. I acted bitchy when I was really afraid, and I questioned whether I loved her [Sandy] or not. I talked about this with [names counselor] and what came out was that I was feeling like I was a failure at sex. We decided to ask Sandy to come to some sessions with me and Sandy agreed to come. I talked about how frightened I was about sex sometimes, and how talk about moving in made that worse. At first, I didn't believe her when she said that for her it wasn't a deal-breaker.

It wasn't clear from Francesca's journal how many counseling sessions involved couple counseling—it seemed there were at least three or four, and that good work was accomplished. Francesca and Sandy were able to separate Francesca's trauma reactions from her more general feelings of love for Sandy (who teased her about the fact that Francesca, being the younger of the two, was making sex an unnecessarily weighty issue).

11. Moseley, "Philosophy of Love," https://iep.utm.edu/love/#H6.

Now consider *philia*, another common and essential form of love:

> In contrast to the desiring and passionate yearning of *eros*, *philia* entails a fondness and appreciation of the other. For the Greeks, the term *philia* incorporated not just friendship, but also loyalties to family and *polis*— one's political community, job, or discipline. . . . The English concept of friendship roughly captures Aristotle's notion of *philia*, as he writes: "things that cause friendship are: doing kindnesses; doing them unasked; and not proclaiming the fact when they are done" (*Rhetoric*, II. 4, trans. Rhys Roberts).
>
> Aristotle elaborates on the kinds of things we seek in proper friendship . . . those who share our dispositions, who bear no grudges, who seek what we do, who are temperate, and just, who admire us appropriately as we admire them, and so on.[12]

Not all depressed people have been as severely traumatized as Francesca, of course. Still, it is common for depression to intrude into intimate relationships in unhelpful ways, and it behooves depressed people to guard against that. Emotional supports have been defined[13] as relationships in which we can discuss emotionally laden issues (vulnerabilities) knowing it is safe to do so and expecting to be understood. The reference above to important couple counseling sessions dealing with Francesca's fears about her sexuality provides a fine example of emotional support in action. As we would expect, it was necessary for her healing that Francesca could access some such relationships—including Sandy, her counselor, and a couple of friends.

She could easily have damaged her relationship to Sandy, and that would potentially have cost her dearly. Depression is, we have said, an alienating condition and because of that it is not unusual for afflicted people to disrupt relationships that they rely on for emotional support and related essential resources:

12. Moseley, "Philosophy of Love," https://iep.utm.edu/love/#H6.
13. See chapter 3.

> [Names counselor] told me more than once that there were two main things I could do to sabotage myself. One thing was to start drinking again and the other was to piss off people who liked me so that I ended up all alone. So far, so good. I feel solid about not drinking these days, and when my depression comes to visit I would rather spend some time alone with it than ragging on to Sandy or my friends that they don't love me enough.

She goes on to discuss a difficult balancing act involving Sandy, their circle of friends, and people at her workplace. On one hand, she needed to recognize times when she had legitimate issues with other people and wanted to talk to them about those; on the other hand, she needed to discern times when she was being unreasonable in her expectations and needed some alone time. Of course, this is something everyone weighs in the relationships they depend upon—it can be more difficult for someone with a history of depression. In any event, it is not, for most, an issue we can manage perfectly and there are usually opportunities for damage control when mistakes are made (revisit chapter 5 about perfectionism):

> After any given depression, there's the need for a lot of cleanup. I remember that I love friends I had thought of letting go. I try to rebuild what I have wasted. After any given depression comes the time to uncrack the eggs and to put the spilled milk back in the container.[14]

Love and God

While love for oneself and for other people (erotic or purely friendly) contribute much to human flourishing, Christians and other people with strong spiritual commitments may yearn for something more, which is "love as an intensely spiritual affair that in its highest permits us to touch divinity:"

> *Agape* refers to the paternal love of God for man and of man for God but is extended to include a brotherly love

14. Solomon, *Noonday Demon*, 70.

for all humanity. . . . *Agape* arguably draws on elements from both *eros* and *philia* in that it seeks a perfect kind of love that is at once a fondness, a transcending of the particular, and a passion without the necessity of reciprocity. The concept is expanded on in the Judaic-Christian tradition of loving God: "You shall love the Lord your God with all your heart, and with all your soul, and with all your might" (Deuteronomy 6:5) and loving "thy neighbour as thyself" (Leviticus 19:18).[15]

We have said that when we compose our narratives about our lives we address five basic questions, among them what we expect from and how we relate to God. One image of God that has traction in our culture is that of the all-powerful and vindictive judge, difficult if not impossible to please and punitive when we fail to meet his exacting standards. This God (usually male) is acutely aware of our many sins while he is relatively unimpressed by our virtues. The consequence of constantly falling woefully short can be eternal damnation. Needless to say, this narrative, if it is embraced, can (and does) fuel depression. How could it do otherwise?

Fortunately, we have alternative narrative options to select from:

> There is another theme that runs through the Bible as a whole, but is especially accented by Jesus. God is neither cosmic ruler nor moral judge. God is love. And Jesus proposes that the image of that love is the love of an infant's father, that is, "Abba." Control and judgment fade into the background; tenderness and unconditional acceptance are central.[16]

Jesus is to be taken seriously, especially his words and example placing love above everything else. Love takes priority in his lessons for us about what we should do to flourish, and a narrative about God's unconditional love belongs at the center of all our stories.

15. Moseley, "Philosophy of Love," https://iep.utm.edu/love/#H6.
16. Cobb, *Jesus' Abba*, Kindle loc. 1898.

Reader Reflections

In a spirit of friendly curiosity, discuss or write about any of the following reflections that look interesting to you:

1. Identify two different narratives about God. Where did you get them from, and how much credibility does each have in your opinion? What do you think the impact of these stories would be on the mood of a depressed person?

2. Did the Greek philosophers' work on types and forms of love contribute anything of value to your thinking?

3. Is self-love necessarily tainted by selfishness and pride? Is this a problem?

4. Some people assert that we cannot love others if we don't love ourselves. Do you agree with this?

5. Why might a depressed person be susceptible to loneliness?

9

Epilogue

We write in order to discover what we think.[1]

The Complex Nature of the Black Dog

IN HIS DESERVEDLY POPULAR book *The Noonday Demon: An Atlas of Depression*, Andrew Solomon describes depression, the "common cold" of mental health problems, as being "overdetermined." His is a book that honors the complexity of its topic, arguing that as common as depression is its causes and treatments are varied, complicated, and far from being fully understood. The search for the causes, the roots of this malady, draws our attention to myriad factors, implicating genetics (and biology more generally), developmental misfortunes like childhood abuse and trauma, sociocultural realties like gender and poverty, and oppression in its various forms (sexism, ageism, racism, domestic violence, spiritual abuse)—a list that could be extended for many lines more.

Andrew Solomon[2] and William Styron[3] are both writers who have penned autobiographical accounts of their own experience

---

1. Variations on this popular thought are variously attributed.

2. Solomon, *Noonday Demon*.

3. Styron, *Darkness Visible*.

with depression, and each likes the familiar snowflake metaphor. Despite being made from the same stuff, no two snowflakes are the same; likewise, no two peoples' experience of depression will ever be identical, however many similarities we see in their unique mix of needs and strengths. In narrative terms, we would not expect two different people to tell the same story without bringing something special and unique to the telling.

The costs depression exacts are enormous, from individuals' suffering through family disruptions, and on up to society at large, which absorbs the cost of lost productivity and creativity, not to mention the expense of providing a variety of professional services.

Our Goals for This Book Revisited

For a problem so large, complicated, and widespread, what can one short book accomplish? Secular service providers (most mental health professionals) are only beginning to appreciate the relevance of religion and spirituality to a significant subset of their clientele—spiritually committed clients in general and Christians specifically. Until recently it was assumed that the important beliefs and values that are part of a Christian client's being in the world could be politely disregarded, left at the consulting room door. Recently this assumption is, in some quarters at least, being questioned with the recognition that a spiritual worldview can be so important that it should be part of the therapeutic conversation.

One hope in writing this book has been to encourage an improved dialogue between Christians with depression and their service providers. If some professionals and their clients come to appreciate more fully the possibility and frequent importance of making faith commitments part of the therapeutic discussion, this book will have accomplished something valuable.

Recent work focused on understanding the lives of religious women experiencing intimate partner violence has demonstrated the need for more effective collaboration between faith leaders and secular helpers[4]; if the present book contributes by encouraging similar sharing of expertise on behalf of Christians with depression, another worthwhile goal will have been achieved. It is often their minister that Christians talk to first when they are troubled, and for her or him to be able to collaborate with secular professionals can be very important.

We have emphasized the importance of depressed people learning to treat themselves affectionately and well; if what we have written encourages a more caring relationship between Christians with depression and their own selves, the work of writing this book will be handsomely rewarded. Sometimes this entails thinking about one's relationship to Christianity itself. We have insisted that Christian beliefs can be good news and bad news, able to exacerbate depression as well as to powerfully help the work required to manage it. We hoped to produce a book that is helpfully honest about some of the pitfalls that can come with a commitment to Christianity at the same time as we are highlighting the blessings it brings.

Reductionism

There is a frequent tendency to be reductionistic about depression, asserting it is nothing but a chemical imbalance in the brain, or repressed anger, or distorted thinking, or unresolved loss, or traumatic life events, or spiritual confusion, or simple loneliness—each of these, or often a combination of any number of causes, can explain depressions.

The reductionistic desire to identify and deal with just one root is understandable, but it is misleading. The late Christian apologist C. S. Lewis called it "nothing buttery," a felicitous phrase describing something we all do when we hope to gain control of problems by oversimplifying them. If depression is nothing but a biochemical brain imbalance, the cure might be a pill; if it is nothing but repressed anger, the cure might be assertiveness training; if

4. Sevcik et al., *Overcoming Conflicting Loyalties.*

it is nothing but helplessness, "positive psychotherapy"[5] might be indicated; if it is nothing but irrational beliefs, CBT might always be the answer.

It's clear that Francesca would be poorly served if she were persuaded that her depression was caused exclusively by a serotonin deficiency, problematic beliefs distorting her relationship to herself and her world, unmet spiritual needs, a side effect of an addiction to alcohol—even just the impact of childhood trauma. In fact, each of these ways of understanding her needs has validity, but none is sufficient in and of itself. Her remarkable resiliency is largely a consequence of her availing herself, over time, of a *package* of services and supports, a package that adequately reflected the complexity of her depression's roots.

Hope

One of the more valuable lessons to be learned from documents like Francesca's journal is the importance of hope, even in the face of very weighty problems. The nurse (in chapter 3) who helped Francesca to recognize symptoms of depression in herself was very likely a busy person, but she found time to reach out to a young alcoholic and that would have been pointless unless she thought there was hope for change.

There were others who put Francesca firmly within their circle of compassion. Where she could have been dismissed as a self-pitying alcoholic (stigma being what it is) there were people who thought she was worthy of compassionate treatment, and they made a difference. Miss Henderson (one of her high school teachers, whom we met in chapter 5) saw and encouraged her love of music, for example. One way and another she was given appropriate medical attention (apparently she was fond of her psychiatrist), she responded to and benefitted from the people running a successful Alcoholics Anonymous program, and she worked with more than one counselor and psychotherapist (one

5. Seligman, *Flourish*.

of whom specialized in the needs of childhood trauma survivors). She valued her job, her relationship with Sandy, a small group of good friends, and her church.

We know that Francesca herself felt hopeless at times, but there was part of her that never gave up, never succumbed to a nihilist's despair. In a late journal entry, she wrote:

> I started off life in a loveless situation, and like most abused kids I was really confused about that. I told [names counselor] that if we could turn the clock back and check me out when I was 13 we would not bet a lot on my chances. I think it was always likely that I would muck things up. It was about that age when I remember sitting up in bed, really scared, thinking I could end up an alcoholic. I have no idea where that thought came from, but it sure scared me.
>
> But my situation now is not at all loveless (Sandy says it never actually was, that God was always there for me). I admit, looking back, that there have been blessings and with help I've sooner or later had the sense to choose what has turned out to be a very good path. I am still surprised by that.
>
> Me being mad at God sometimes is only part of the story. I also know I've been helped a lot, and I'm thankful for that. These days I don't want to be anybody other than me. That surprises me too, but it's a fact.

Bibliography

American Psychiatric Association. *Diagnostic and Statistical Manual of Mental Disorders.* 5th ed. Arlington, VA: American Psychiatric Association, 2013.

Arieti, Silvano, and Jules Bemporad. *Severe and Mild Depression: The Psychotherapeutic Approach.* New York: Basic Books, 1978.

Ayed, Nahlah. "'I Love You': The Most Treasured (and Misunderstood) Expression of All Time." Podcast. Ideas 2020. https://www.cbc.ca/listen/live-radio/1-23-ideas/clip/15761034-i-love-you-treasured-and-misunderstood-expression.

Baldwin, Christina. *Life's Companion: Journal Writing as a Spiritual Practice.* London: Random House, 1990.

Birnbaum, Jack. *Cry Anger.* Don Mills, ON: General Publishing, 1973.

Borg, Marcus J. *The Heart of Christianity: Rediscovering a Life of Faith.* San Francisco: HarperSanFrancisco, 2003.

————. *Speaking Christian: Why Christian Words Have Lost Their Meaning and Power—and How They Can Be Restored.* Epub ed. New York: HarperCollins, 2011.

Brown, Brené. *The Gifts of Imperfection.* Center City, MI: Hazelden, 2010.

Brown, Valerie. *Living from the Center: Mindfulness Meditation and Centering for Friends* Pamphlet 407. Kindle ed. Wallingford, PA: Pendle Hill, 2010.

Bryant-Davis, Thelma, and Eunice C. Wong. "Faith to Move Mountains: Religious Coping, Spirituality, and Interpersonal Trauma Recovery." *American Psychologist,* November 2013, 675–84.

Buber, Martin. *I and Thou.* Translated by Walter Kaufmann. New York: Scribner, 1970.

Cameron, Gary. "The Potential of Informal Social Support Strategies in Child Welfare." In *Child Maltreatment: Expanding Our Concept of Helping,* edited by Michael Rothery and Gary Cameron, 145–67. Hillsdale, NJ: Lawrence Erlbaum, 1990.

Canda, Edward. *Spiritual Diversity in Social Work Practice: The Heart of Helping.* 3rd ed. New York: Oxford University Press, 2019.

Caputo, John D. *The Weakness of God: A Theology of the Event.* Bloomington, IN: Indiana University Press, 2006.

Chandon, John S, Tom Thomas, Krishna M Gokhale, Siddhartha Bandyopadhyay, Julie Taylor, and Krishnarajah Nirantharakumar. "The

Burden of Mental Ill Health Associated with Childhood Maltreatment in the UK, Using the Health Improvement Network Database: A Population-Based Retrospective Cohort Study." *Lancet Psychiatry*, September 26, 2019, 1–9.

Cipriani, Andrea, Toshi A. Furukawa, Georgia Salanti, Anna Charimani, Lauren Z. Atkinson, Yusuke Ogawa, Stephan Leucht, et al. "Comparative Efficacy and Acceptability of 21 Antidepressant Drugs for the Acute Treatment of Adults with Major Depressive Disorder: A Systematic Review and Network Meta-Analysis." *The Lancet*, February 21, 2018. https://doi.org/10.1016/S0140-6736(17)32802-7.

Clayton, Philip. *Religion and Science: The Basics*. New York: Routledge, 2012.

Cobb, John B. Jr. *Jesus' Abba: The God Who Has Not Failed*. Kindle ed. Minneapolis: Augsburg Fortress, 2015.

Courtois, Christine A., and Julian D. Ford. *Treatment of Complex Trauma: A Sequenced, Relationship-Based Approach*. New York: Guilford, 2013.

Cregan, Mary. *The Scar: A Personal History of Depression and Recovery*. New York: Norton, 2019.

Csikszentmihalyi, Mihaly. *Creativity: Flow and the Psychology of Discovery and Invention*. New York: HarperCollins, 1998.

Dalai Lama, Desmond Tutu, and Douglas Abrams. *The Book of Joy: Lasting Happiness in a Changing World*. New York: Penguin Random House, 2016.

Dawkins, Richard. *River Out of Eden: A Darwinian View of Life*. New York: Basic Books, 1995.

Diederich, F. Remy. *Broken Trust: A Practical Guide to Identify Toxic Faith, Toxic Church, and Spiritual Abuse*. The Overcoming Series. Kindle ed. Amazon, 2017.

Doyle, Thomas P. "The Spiritual Trauma Experienced by Victims of Sexual Abuse by Catholic Clergy." *Pastoral Psychology* 58 (2009) 239–60.

Fawcett, Sharon L. *Hope for Wholeness: The Spiritual Path to Freedom from Depression*. Colorado Springs, CO: Navpress, 2008.

Finley, James. *Christian Meditation: Experiencing the Presence of God*. New York: HarperCollins, 2004.

Flaherty, Sandra M. *Woman, Why Do You Weep? Spirituality for Survivors of Childhood Sexual Abuse*. New York: Paulist, 1992.

Frankl, Viktor E. *Man's Search for Meaning*. New York: Washington Square, 1984.

———. *Man's Search for Ultimate Meaning*. 3rd ed. New York: Basic Books, 2000.

Fromm, Erich. *The Art of Loving*. New York: Open Road Integrated Media, 2013.

Gatta, Julia. *Life in Christ: Practicing Christian Spirituality*. New York: Church Publishing, 2018.

Gebka, Robert. *Managing Depression with Mindfulness for Dummies*. Chichester, West Sussex, UK: John Wiley, 2016.

Green, Jim. *Giving Up without Giving Up: Meditation and Depressions*. Kindle ed. London: Bloomsbury Continuum, 2019.

Greenblatt, Stephen. *The Rise and Fall of Adam and Eve*. New York: Norton, 2017.

Greenson, Ralph R. *The Technique and Practice of Psychoanalysis*. New York: International Universities Press, 1967.

Griffith, James L. *Religion That Heals, Religion That Harms: A Guide for Clinical Practice*. New York: Guilford, 2010.

Griswold, Charles L. *Forgiveness: A Philosophical Exploration*. New York: Cambridge University Press, 2007.

Hägglund, Martin. *This Life: Secular Faith and Spiritual Freedom*. Kindle ed. New York: Pantheon, 2019.

Hari, Johann. *Lost Connections: Uncovering the Real Causes of Depression—and the Unexpected Solutions*. Kindle ed. New York: Bloomsbury, 2018.

Harries, Richard. *The Beauty and the Horror: Searching for God in a Suffering World*. Kindle ed. London: SPCK, 2016.

Heller, Rick. *Secular Meditation: 32 Practices for Cultivating Inner Peace, Compassion, and Joy*. Novato, CA: New World Library, 2015.

Herman, Judith. *Trauma and Recovery: The Aftermath of Violence— from Domestic Abuse to Political Terror*. Kindle ed. New York: Basic Books, 2015.

Hieronymus, F., J. F. Emilsson, S. Nilsson, and E. Eriksson. "Consistent Superiority of Selective Serotonin Reuptake Inhibitors over Placebo in Reducing Depressed Mood in Patients with Major Depression." *Molecular Psychiatry* 21 (2016) 523–30.

Hodge, David R. *Spiritual Assessment in Social Work and Mental Health Practice*. New York: Columbia University Press, 2015.

Holloway, Richard. *On Forgiveness: How Can We Forgive the Unforgiveable?* Edinburgh, UK: Cannongate, 2002.

hooks, bell. *All About Love: New Visions*. Ebook ed. New York: HarperCollins, 2000.

Jones, James W. *The Mirror of God: Christian Faith as Spiritual Practice— Lessons from Buddhism and Psychotherapy*. Kindle ed. New York: Palgrave MacMillan, 2003.

Kira, I. A. "Etiology and Treatment of Post-Cumulative Traumatic Stress Disorders in Different Cultures." *Traumatology* 16/4 (2010) 128–41.

Kramer, Peter D. *Against Depression*. London: Viking, 2005.

Kushner, Harold S. *When Bad Things Happen to Good People*. New York: Anchor, 2004.

Laird, Martin. *An Ocean of Light: Contemplation, Transformation, and Liberation*. New York: Oxford University Press, 2019.

———. *A Sunlit Absence: Silence, Awareness, and Contemplation*. New York: Oxford University Press, 2011.

Lehrer, Jonah. *Imagine: How Creativity Works*. Kindle ed. Toronto: Allen Lane, 2012.

Lloyd-Jones, D. Martyn. *Spiritual Depression: Its Causes and Cure.* Grand Rapids: Eerdmans, 1965.

Long, Thomas G. *What Shall We Say?: Evil, Suffering, and the Crisis of Faith.* Kindle ed. Grand Rapids: Eerdmans, 2011.

MacCulloch, Diarmaid. *Christianity: The First Three Thousand Years.* Kindle ed. New York: Penguin, 2009.

Marotta-Walters, Sylvia A. "Spiritual Meaning Making Following Clergy-Perpetrated Sexual Abuse." *Traumatology* 21/2 (2015) 64–70.

McConnaughey, Janyne. *Brave: A Personal Story of Healing Childhood Trauma.* Kindle ed. Greeley, CO: Cladach, 2018.

———. *Jeannie's Brave Childhood: Behavior and Healing through the Lens of Attachment and Trauma.* Kindle ed. Greeley, CO: Cladach, 2019.

Merkin, Daphne. *This Close to Happy: A Reckoning with Depression.* New York: Farrar, Straus and Giroux, 2017.

Merton, Thomas. *Conjectures of a Guilty Bystander.* Garden City, NY: Doubleday, 1966.

———. *Contemplative Prayer.* New York: Doubleday, 1969.

Miller, Arthur. *After the Fall.* Kindle ed. New York: Penguin, 1980.

Moltmann, Jürgen. "Christianity: A Religion of Joy." In *Joy and Human Flourishing: Essays on Theology, Culture, and the Good Life*, edited by Miroslav Volf and Justin E. Crisp, 1–16. Minneapolis: Fortress, 2015.

Moseley, Alexander. "Philosophy of Love." *Internet Encyclopedia of Philosophy*, edited by James Feiser and Bradley Dowden. https://iep.utm.edu/love/#H6.

Murray, David P. *Christians Get Depressed Too: Hope and Help for Depressed People.* Kindle ed. Grand Rapids: Reformation Heritage, 2010.

Nussbaum, Martha. *Anger and Forgiveness: Resentment, Generosity, Justice.* New York: Oxford University Press, 2016.

———. *Creating Capabilities: The Human Development Approach.* Cambridge, MA: Harvard University Press, 2011.

———. *Upheavals of Thought: The Intelligence of Emotions.* Cambridge, UK: Cambridge University Press, 2001.

O'Loughlin, Michael. "Pennsylvania Report Documents over 1,000 Victims of Priest Abuse." *The Jesuit Review*, August 14, 2018.

Oord, Thomas Jay. *God Can't: How to Believe in God and Love after Tragedy, Abuse, or Other Evils.* Kindle ed. Grasmere, ID: Sacrasage, 2019.

———. *The Uncontrolling Love of God: An Open and Relational Account of Providence.* Downers Grove, IL: InterVarsity 2015.

Palmer, Parker. "All the Way Down: Depression and the Spiritual Journey." *Weavings* 13 (September/October 1998) 31–41.

Pargament, Kenneth I. *Spiritually Integrated Psychotherapy: Understanding and Addressing the Sacred.* New York: Guilford, 2007.

Pearce, Michelle. *Cognitive Behavioral Therapy for Christians with Depression: A Practical Tool-Based Primer.* West Conshohocken, PA: Templeton, 2016.

Peck, M. Scott. *The Road Less Travelled: A New Psychology of Love, Traditional Values, and Spiritual Growth.* New York: Simon and Schuster, 1978.

Pennington, Jonathan T. *The Sermon on the Mount and Human Flourishing: A Theological Commentary.* Grand Rapids: Baker Academic, 2017.

Pennington, M. Basil, Thomas Keating, and Thomas Clarke. *Finding Grace at the Center: The Beginning of Centering Prayer.* 3rd ed. Kindle ed. Woodstock, VT: Skylight Paths, 2007.

Rhodes, James. *Instrumental: A Memoir of Madness, Medication, and Music.* New York: Bloomsbury, 2014.

Roper, Lyndal. *Martin Luther: Renegade and Prophet.* London: Bodley Head, 2016.

Rothery, Michael. "Critical Ecological Systems Theory." In *Theoretical Perspectives for Direct Social Work Practice: A Generalist-Eclectic Approach* 3rd ed. Edited by Nick F. Coady and Peter Lehmann, 81–107. New York: Springer, 2016.

———. "Family Therapy with Multiproblem Families." In *Child Maltreatment: Expanding Our Concept of Helping,* edited by Michael Rothery and Gary Cameron, 1–9. Hillsdale, NJ: Lawrence Erlbaum, 1990.

Runco, Mark A. "Creativity." *Annual Review of Psychology* 55 (2004) 657–87.

Segal, Zindel, Mark Williams, and John Teasdale. *Mindfulness-Based Cognitive Therapy for Depression.* 2nd ed. New York: Guilford, 2013.

Seligman, Martin E. P. "Explanatory Style: Predicting Depression, Achievement and Health." In *Brief Therapy Approaches to Treating Anxiety and Depression,* edited by Michael D. Yapko, 5–32. New York: Brunner/Mazel, 1989.

———. *Flourish: A Visionary New Understanding of Happiness and Well-Being.* New York: Atria, 2011.

———. *The Hope Circuit: A Psychologist's Journey from Helplessness to Optimism.* New York: Public Affairs, 2018.

———. *Learned Optimism: How to Change Your Mind and Your Life.* New York: Vintage, 1990.

Sevcik, Irene, Michael Rothery, Nancy Nason-Clark, and Robert Pynn. *Overcoming Conflicting Loyalties: Intimate Partner Violence, Community Resources, and Faith.* Edmonton: University of Alberta Press, 2015.

Solomon, Andrew. *The Noonday Demon.* New York: Scribner, 2001.

Styron, William. *Darkness Visible: A Memoir of Madness.* New York: Vintage, 1990.

Suchocki, Marjorie Hewitt. *The Fall to Violence: Original Sin in Relational Theology.* New York: Continuum, 1994.

Suddendorf, Thomas. *The Gap: The Science of What Separates Us from Other Animals.* New York: Basic Books, 2013.

Tobin, Theresa W. "Religious Faith in the Unjust Meantime: The Spiritual Violence of Clergy Sexual Abuse." *Feminist Philosophy Quarterly* 5/2 (2019) 1–29.

Van der Kolk, Bessel A. *The Body Keeps the Score: Brain, Mind, and Body in the Healing of Trauma.* Kindle ed. New York: Penguin, 2014.

Van der Kolk, Bessel A., and Rita Fisler. "Dissociation and the Fragmentary Nature of Traumatic Memories: Overview and Exploratory Study." *Journal of Traumatic Stress* 8 (1995) 505–25. http://www.trauma-pages.com/vanderk2.htm.

Volf, Miroslav. "The Crown of the Good Life: A Hypothesis." In *Joy and Human Flourishing: Essays on Theology, Culture, and the Good Life,* edited by Miroslav Volf and Justin E. Crisp, 127–35. Minneapolis: Fortress, 2015.

———. *Flourishing: Why We Need Religion in a Globalized World.* New Haven, CT: Yale University Press, 2015.

Winnette, Petra, and Jonathan Baylin. *Working with Traumatic Memories to Heal Adults with Unresolved Childhood Trauma: Neuroscience, Attachment Theory and Pesso Boyden System Psychomotor Psychotherapy.* Kindle ed. London: Jessica Kingsley, 2017.

Wittgenstein, Ludwig. *Philosophical Investigations: The German Text, with a Revised English Translation.* Translated by G. E. M. Anscombe. 3rd (50th anniversary commemorative) ed. Oxford, UK: Blackwell, 2001.

Yinger, Kent L. *God and Human Wholeness: Perfection in Biblical and Theological Tradition.* Eugene, OR: Cascade, 2019.